Animals
of Kruger
National Park

Keith Barnes

PRINCETON
press.princeton.edu

Published by Princeton University Press,
41 William Street, Princeton, New Jersey 08540
In the United Kingdom: Princeton University Press, 6 Oxford Street,
Woodstock, Oxfordshire OX20 1TR
nathist.press.princeton.edu

Requests for permission to reproduce material from this work should be sent to
Permissions, Princeton University Press

First published 2016

British Library Cataloging-in-Publication Data is available

Library of Congress Control Number 2016930333
ISBN 978-0-691-16178-5

Production and design by **WILD**Guides Ltd., Old Basing, Hampshire UK.
Printed in China

10 9 8 7 6 5 4 3 2 1

*This book is dedicated to my parents, who instilled
a passion for nature in a young man, and my wife
Yi-fang and son Joshua, for putting up with it in
an older one.*

*And to Pierre and Eve Cronje, who helped my
family through a difficult time.*

Contents

The region 7
The aim of this book 8
How to use this book 10
Glossary of terms 12
Kruger's importance for biodiversity 14
The seasons and timing your visit 15
Considerations for your visit 16
The habitats 17
Characteristic plants 18
Map showing the distribution of habitats in Kruger National Park 22
Map of Kruger National Park and adjacent private concession areas
    forming the Greater Kruger National Park conservation area 23
How, where and when to watch animals in Kruger National Park 24
The ten best wildlife-watching routes 28

MAMMALS 31
Mammal tracks 32
Lion Panthera leo 40
Leopard Panthera pardus 44
Cheetah Acinonyx jubatus 48
Serval Leptailurus serval 52
Caracal Caracal caracal 53
Wild Cat Felis sylvestris 54
African Civet Civettictis civetta 55
Common Genet Genetta genetta 56
Large-spotted Genet Genetta maculata 57
Spotted Hyena Crocuta crocuta 58
Aardwolf Proteles cristata 62
Banded Mongoose Mungos mungo 64
Common Dwarf Mongoose Helogale parvula 65
Common Slender Mongoose Herpestes sanguineus 66
White-tailed Mongoose Ichneumia albicauda 67
Zorilla Ictonyx striatus 68
Honey Badger Mellivora capensis 69
Black-backed Jackal Canis mesomelas 70
Side-striped Jackal Canis adustus 71
African Wild Dog Lycaon pictus 72
Temminck's Ground Pangolin Smutsia temminckii 74
Aardvark Orycteropus afer 75
Spotted-necked Otter Hydrictis maculicollis 76
African Clawless Otter Aonyx capensis 77
African Elephant Loxodonta africana 78
White Rhinoceros Ceratotherium simum 82
Black Rhinoceros Diceros bicornis 84
Hippopotamus Hippopotamus amphibious 86
Common Warthog Phacochoerus africanus 90
Plains Zebra Equus quagga 92
Giraffe Giraffa camelopardalis 94
African Buffalo Syncerus caffer 98
Common Eland Tragelaphus oryx 102
Greater Kudu Tragelaphus strepsiceros 104
Common Duiker Sylvicapra grimmia 106

Sharpe's Grysbok *Raphicerus sharpei* 107
Steenbok *Raphicerus campestris* 108
Klipspringer *Oreotragus oreotragus* 109
Southern Reedbuck *Redunca arundinum* 110
Bushbuck *Tragelaphus scriptus* 112
Nyala *Tragelaphus angasii* 114
Roan Antelope *Hippotragus equinus* 116
Sable Antelope *Hippotragus niger* 118
Waterbuck *Kobus ellipsiprymnus* 120
Impala *Aepyceros melampus* 122
Tsessebe *Damaliscus lunatus* 124
Common Wildebeest *Connochaetes taurinus* 126
Scrub Hare *Lepus saxatilis* 128
Springhare *Pedetes capensis* 129
Rock Hyrax *Procavia capensis* 130
Cape Porcupine *Hystrix africaeaustralis* 131
Vervet (Monkey) *Chlorocebus pygerythrus* 132
Chacma Baboon *Papio ursinus* 134
Southern Lesser Galago *Galago moholi* 136
Thick-tailed Greater Galago *Otolemur crassicaudatus* 137
Smith's Bush Squirrel *Paraxerus cepapi* 138
Epauletted fruit-bats *Epomophorus* spp. 139

REPTILES 140
Nile Crocodile *Crocodylus niloticus* 142
Leopard Tortoise *Stigmochelys pardalis* 144
Serrated Hinged Terrapin *Pelusios sinuatus* 145
Water Monitor *Varanus niloticus* 146
Rock Monitor *Varanus albigularis* 146
Puff Adder *Bitis arietans* 148
Mozambique Spitting Cobra *Naja mossambica* 149
Black Mamba *Dendroaspis polylepis* 150
Southern African Python *Python natalensis* 151
Common Flap-necked Chameleon *Chamaeleo dilepis* 152
Southern Tree Agama *Acanthocercus atricollis* 153
Rainbow Skink *Trachylepis margaritifer* 154
Striped Skink *Trachylepis striata* 155
Variable Skink *Trachylepis varia* 156
Common Tropical House Gecko *Hemidactylus mabouia* 157
Common Giant Plated Lizard *Matobosaurus validus* 158
Rough-scaled Plated Lizard *Broadleysaurus major* 159

AMPHIBIANS 160
African Bullfrog *Pyxicephalus edulis* 162
Southern Foam-nest Frog *Chiromantis xerampelina* 163
Banded Rubber Frog *Phrynomantis bifasciatus* 164
Snoring Puddle Frog *Phrynobatrachus natalensis* 165
Bubbling Kassina *Kassina senegalensis* 166
Plain Grass Frog *Ptychadena anchietae* 167
Bushveld Rain Frog *Breviceps adspersus* 168
Painted Reed Frog *Hyperolius marmoratus* 169

Further reading and online resources 170
South African National Parks (SANParks) main regulations 171
Rhinos on the edge 172
Acknowledgements and photo credits 173
Index 174

The region

The very name 'Kruger' immediately conjures up a sense of untouched naturalness and the timeless existence of unimaginable generations of animals and other creatures of impressive variety. Whilst the extreme horizons bear witness to the vastness of the park, it is the thought of the wonderful wildlife it sustains that excites the visitor when eyes are first laid upon the great plains or extensive swathes of woodland. Whether one's passion is for the huge, lumbering elephants or the most insignificant of insects, the sheer complexity of life in this stunning setting will leave a lifetime's impression with the first-time visitor.

At 20,000 km², Kruger National Park's extent is impressive in itself, about the size of Wales and just a little smaller than Belize – but combined with a number of private concessions and reserves to the west, the wilderness area is expanded to nearly 22,000 km². The Kruger sits south and west of the Gonarezhou National Park in Zimbabwe and Limpopo National Park in Mozambique, collectively known as the Great Limpopo Transfrontier Park, which contributes another 35,000 km² of protected land mass. If future plans to expand the protected area to include the Banhine and Zinave National Parks in Mozambique come to pass, a conservation area of nearly 100,000 km² will have been created.

Whilst the many sights, sounds and experiences that await the visitor to the Kruger National Park are the main subject of this book, it is sufficiently broad in scope to cover the fauna found in any of these adjacent areas.

The expansiveness of Kruger is easily admired from lookout points like the one at Olifants Rest Camp.

The aim of this book

Twenty years ago, the average visitor to Kruger National Park was only interested in seeing the 'Big 5' mammals. Now, many of the nearly 1·4 million visitors streaming into the park each year have a broader interest in wildlife – often sparked after, for example, seeing a cute Common Dwarf Mongoose at one of the camps, or a spectacular Southern Tree Agama bobbing its head up and down in display. Of course, in this book, the famous 'megafauna' of Kruger features prominently, but the coverage is much wider than that, allowing you to identify most of the mammals and the more common reptiles and frogs that you are likely to encounter on a 1–2 week visit to Kruger or the adjacent reserves. Although birds are a visible and frequently encountered group of animals – with over 500 species recorded in the park – they are not covered in this book but instead are the subject of a separate, companion guide *Birds of Kruger National Park* (see *page 170*). So if your interest extends to birds, these two books make a great set.

Kruger supports around 148 species of mammals, 118 reptiles and 35 amphibians. However, these figures include dozens of nocturnal bats, mice and frogs that are rarely observed by most visitors. Rather than covering all these species and creating a cumbersome book that is difficult to use in the field, the focus here is on the animals that are most likely

Cheetahs mating. Although this book is an aid to identifying animals, it also provides information on habits, habitat preferences, diet, breeding behaviour, and social structure; it is therefore an invaluable reference for understanding the biology of Kruger's animals.

to be encountered, or are particularly sought-after. The result is a compact book featuring 57 types of mammals, 17 reptiles and eight amphibians. It is designed to be intuitive for those new to identifying animals, and as far as possible avoids the use of jargon and complex scientific terms – although a short glossary has been provided (*page 12*) to explain the few that have been used. Information on behaviour and biology is included to help enrich your wildlife watching experience beyond just knowing what you are looking at.

The introductory sections of the book aim to help you plan your visit by providing information on timing your visit (*page 15*), the choice of camp and other considerations (*page 16*), how, where and when to watch animals (*page 24*), and suggestions of the routes to follow that are likely to give you the best chances of encountering Kruger's amazing wildlife (*page 28*). The result is a lightweight, easy-to-carry guide, packed with information and instructive photographs. As such, it is a very handy reference for those new to safari-going, as well those who are regular visitors, and the hope is that it inspires more people to appreciate, understand and enjoy the wonderful and fascinating wildlife of the park.

It is possible that you may encounter some species on your visit that are not included in this book. If you want to find out more, the *Further reading* section (*page 170*) provides suggestions of other books to flesh-out your wildlife library.

The **Impala Lily** is spectacular and can brighten the dry savannah.

How to use this book

Taxonomy, the science of naming and categorizing animals and plants, is complex and ever-changing. Many books that deal with the identification of safari animals will stick to the strict order of one scientific authority or another, but in this book the animals are ordered in a more intuitive and user-friendly fashion. The most sought-after group, the cats, is covered first, followed by the other mammalian predators, then the ungulates, and finally a motley assortment including the primates, hares and others. The reptiles and frogs follow, ordered from the most easily recognized to the most obscure. As far as possible, animals that resemble each other are placed close together; for example, the Rock Hyrax is near the hares and Springhare, rather than next to its closest relative, the African Elephant.
All the species covered are listed on the contents pages in the order in which they appear. For ease of reference, a short index to the main animal groups is on the inside back cover. This is in addition to the full index which includes both the common and scientific names (and alternative names, where relevant) of every species mentioned in the text.

To standardize the scientific and English names used in the book, the well-respected International Union for Conservation of Nature (IUCN) has been followed for the mammals. For the reptiles and amphibians, the Animal Demography Unit's (ADU) Virtual Museum database (http://vmus.adu.org.za) is followed. This reflects the latest taxonomic thinking by southern Africa's reptile and frog experts. Each species is given a common name (in **bold text**) and scientific name (in *italicized text*).

The IUCN Red List categories, summarized below, are widely used to prioritize the species that need conservation action. It is a sobering fact that of the 57 mammal species included in this book, seven are globally threatened (Critically Endangered, Endangered or Vulnerable) and four are Near Threatened; this is highlighted in the relevant species accounts (see www.iucnredlist.org for more information). None of the reptile or frog species featured in this book are globally threatened.

Critically Endangered	Faces an extremely high risk of extinction in the wild.
Endangered	Faces a very high risk of extinction in the wild.
Vulnerable	Considered to be facing a high risk of extinction in the wild.
Near Threatened	Likely to be qualify for a globally threatened category (at least Vulnerable) in the near future.

For each species in the book there is a table that summarises key information on its identification and biology, as explained below:

Size	The size given is either: **TL (total length)** – as measured from the tip of the nose to the tip of the tail; or **HB (head and body)** – the length of the animal from the tip of the nose to the base of the tail; and **Tail** – the length of the tail. Where male (♂) and female (♀) differ, separate measurements are given. Measurements are given in metres (m) or centimetres (cm).
Weight	The weight of the animal in tonnes, kilogrammes (kg) or grammes (g); where different, weight ranges for males (♂) and females (♀) are given separately (or an indication of which sex is the heavier). If appropriate, the maximum recorded weight is also given.
Key identification features	The diagnostic features that identify a species, and where appropriate the differences from similar species.
Habitat	The habitat(s) in which the animal is most likely to be encountered.
Habits	Synopsis of the species' daily activity patterns, social structure and/or behaviour.
Diet	Summary of the animal's diet.

The main text in each species account covers the animal's status in Kruger, how to tell it from similar species (if any), and interesting facts about its biology. This will vary according to species and may also include information about the animal's natural history and/or conservation.

To help you keep track of what you have seen, a small box has been included next to the animal's name so that you can tick it off as you go.

Kruger has a massive population of **African Elephant** and large groups are frequently encountered.

Glossary of terms

alpha	dominant male, female or pair
aestivate	a state of dormancy (torpor) during a hot or dry period
boss	a knob-like swelling at the base of the horns of certain animals (*e.g.* African Buffalo, Common Wildebeest)
carnivore (carnivorous)	a species that feeds mainly or exclusively on animal tissue, whether through predation or scavenging (see also **herbivore, insectivore, omnivore**)
clan	an extended family group of related animals
coalesce	to form a **coalition** (see below)
coalition	a group of animals that cooperates for a common purpose
crepuscular	active at twilight (dawn and dusk)
diagnostic	a distinctive or unique feature that enables confident identification
dimorphic	two distinct forms within a species, *e.g.* sexually dimorphic, where the male and female look different
diurnal	active during daylight
dorsal	the upper surface – usually the back of an animal
extant	still in existence (as opposed to **extinct**)
extinct	a biological group (species, genus, lineage) that has no living individuals
faeces	waste matter from digested food (*e.g.* scat, dung, droppings)
forage	to search for food
gestation	the time spent in the womb between conception and birth
grizzled	the appearance of being streaked with greyish (salt-and-pepper) hair
harem	a group of female animals that share a single male mate
herbivore (herbivorous)	a species that feeds mainly or exclusively on plant material, *e.g.* leaves, grass, bark as opposed to fruit (see also **carnivore, insectivore, omnivore**)
infanticide	the killing of young, often as a strategy to stimulate females to enter breeding condition
insectivore (insectivorous)	a species that feeds mainly or exclusively on insects – other species that are not insectivorous may also eat insects as supplementary protein, but only during certain periods, *e.g.* breeding (see also **carnivore, herbivore, omnivore**)
invertebrate	an animal lacking a backbone (*e.g.* insects, worms, spiders)
kopje (inselberg)	small hill in an area of open plains
litter	a group of young born at the same time

masculine	male characteristics or qualities
mate-guard	where one sex (normally the male) attempts to prevent a chosen mate from mating with its rivals
megafauna	large mammals
midden	a pile of dung/faeces
monogamous	having only a single mate at any one time (see also **polygamous**)
nepotism	favouring a closely related individual
nocturnal	active during the night (see also **crepuscular**)
oestrus	the period when a female mammal is sexually receptive and able to conceive
omnivore (omnivorous)	a species that habitually feeds on both animal (including insects) and plant material (including fruit and fungi)
pan	a natural basin or depression in the earth that often contains open mud or water
penis	the male genital organ used for copulation
polygamous	having multiple mates at any one time
ruminant	an even-toed ungulate mammal that chews the cud regurgitated from its rumen. The ruminants comprise cattle, antelopes, giraffes, and their relatives
ruminate	to bring up and chew again food that has already been chewed and swallowed (the cud)
rut	the season of heightened sexual activity in male **ruminants**
saddle	the back and sides of an animal behind the neck and in front of the rump
savannah	an area of grassland and woodland in tropical regions
scrotum	external sack of skin enclosing the testicles of most male mammals
spoor	the track, scent or scat (see **faeces**) left by an animal
tactile	relating to the sense of touch
taxonomy	the scientific study of naming species and classifying the relationships between them
terrestrial	a preference for living on the ground
territorial	consistently defending a territory from intruders of the same (and in some cases other) species
testosterone	male steroid hormone that drives the development of adult male characteristics in mammals
thermoregulation	the process of gaining or losing heat in order to maintain a constant internal body temperature
vertebrate	animal with a backbone: fish, amphibian, reptile, bird or mammal

Kruger's importance for biodiversity

Kruger is justly famous for its incredible populations of the 'Big 5' large mammals which attract visitors from far and wide. The 'Big 5' are Lion, Leopard, African Buffalo, African Elephant and 'Rhinoceros' (actually two species – Black Rhinoceros and White Rhinoceros (hereafter referred to as Rhinos)). But the park is much more than that. Kruger is home to a staggering diversity of plants and animals (biodiversity), including some 335 tree species, 49 fishes, 118 reptiles, 35 amphibians, 148 mammals and more than 500 birds, making it one of the richest conservation areas in the world. Also, because of its huge area, it supports significant numbers of the animals that occur within its boundaries, many of which are threatened species. For example, Kruger currently has the largest remaining population of White Rhino (although poaching is a massive problem (see *page 85*)), and very important populations of predators such as Cheetah, Lion and African Wild Dog, as well as both Roan and Sable Antelopes. Kruger also supports a phenomenal 60% of the bird species that have been recorded in South Africa, and, perhaps more importantly, a staggering 32 species of globally threatened and Near Threatened birds. Within a South African context, sizeable populations of some large and localized reptiles are found in Kruger, including Southern African Python and Nile Crocodile.

All in all, Kruger is a prize asset and vital haven for a huge proportion of South Africa's wildlife. Fortunately, it is also an institution for many South Africans, as well as international visitors who are fond patrons of the park. In fact, Kruger is such a commercial success that it funds much of the national park operations elsewhere in South Africa, where parks in areas that are seldom visited but rich in biodiversity, such as the Karoo region, struggle to pay for themselves. Indeed, the success of Kruger has made it the heart and soul of South African National Park's biodiversity conservation efforts.

Large mammals and small insects often rely on each other in some way. Here a **dung beetle** rolls away a dropping for use as a chamber into which it lays its eggs. When these hatch, the emerging larvae have a readily available source of food.

The seasons and timing your visit

The climate is characterized by two distinct seasons: a hot and wet rainy period that extends from October to March, and a cool and dry period from April to September. Kruger receives an average annual rainfall of about 550 mm, with the highest rainfall ranging from 625–750 mm in the southwest around Pretoriuskop, and the lowest ranging from 375–550 mm in the northeast near Pafuri and Shingwedzi. The average daily minimum and maximum temperatures are 9·5–26·1°C in winter and 22·4–32·4°C in summer. While there is probably no bad time to visit Kruger, some times of the year are better than others and you should try to time your visit based on your interests.

The best time is generally in autumn, winter and early spring (April to September). During this period the vegetation is dry, there have been a few winter fires, and the habitat is much more open – which makes the animals easier to see. It is also the time when animals are drawn to permanent water sources such as waterholes and rivers, which makes them easier to locate. The weather also tends to be sunny, humidity is low, temperatures are mild, and there is a lower risk of contracting malaria. If you plan to visit at that time, it is a good idea to check exactly when the mid-year South African school holiday break falls, as you will need to book well in advance. The only negatives associated with this season are that it can be a little dusty, the open-vehicle drives can be cold, and for photographers the dry savannah with little greenery can make landscapes less attractive.

By October and November the rains will have begun, and although the bush will have started to thicken and animals started to disperse more widely, this can be an optimal time for the wildlife photographer. Many animals give birth at this time to coincide with the growth of new grass and the greener, lusher backdrop offers different photo opportunities. Birds and frogs are also at their peak during this period, and easily combined with a fantastic safari experience. From December to March it is mid-summer and the temperatures and humidity increase dramatically, regularly reaching over 35°C and 40–70% respectively. The long summer school holidays in December and January make for an extremely crowded park, and with the bush greening up and water widespread, the animals disperse and are much harder to locate. This is also the peak time for malarial mosquitoes in Kruger. On the positive side, the birding and photography opportunities are very good during this period.

After the wet season rains, birds and frogs are attracted to temporary pools and flooded grassland, making this a great time to visit if you interested in more than the big mammals.

Considerations for your visit

Once you have decided when to visit Kruger, the next consideration is where to stay. The choice ranges from luxury lodges (some of the finest in Africa are nestled in the private reserves adjacent to the park) to more moderate places with self-catering accommodation. Booking a luxury travel experience at the private concessions on the western border of the park could well provide one of the finest wilderness experiences of your life – although of course this does come at a cost. These lodges have impeccable ethics in terms of the management of game-viewing encounters: for example, not more than three vehicles normally being permitted at a single sighting. One of the main advantages of visiting private concessions is that the rangers have permission to drive off-road, which maximizes your chances of close encounters with cats such as Leopards, or fast-moving African Wild Dogs. Combined with amazing food and fabulous accommodation, these camps often cannot be beaten. There are also many companies that run trips into the government-run sector of Kruger that are worth considering; details of these companies are easily found online.

Alternatively, Kruger offers probably the very best do-it-yourself safari experience on the planet. Camp accommodation can be booked online (www.sanparks.org; email: reservations@sanparks.org). If you are planning on spending more than ten days a year in South African National Parks it is worth obtaining a Wild Card – an annual pass to most of the country's state parks and reserves. There are daily flights from South Africa's international hub in Johannesburg (O. R. Tambo Airport) to Skukuza, Palaborwa and Hoedspruit airports. Cars can be hired, and self-drive is straightforward. Tall vehicles with good ground clearance are likely to be best for game viewing and it is also possible to hire open-vehicles from safari operators near the park – but although the latter are fantastic for game viewing, you will be exposed to the elements during cold or inclement weather.

If you have already been on several safaris and are looking for an alternative approach, consider a multiple-day walking safari with an experienced tracker and guide. This will give you a completely different bush experience.

The private camps adjacent to Kruger offer unrivalled encounters with wildlife, and an element of intimacy that is unbeatable.

The habitats

Kruger's geology is complex, resulting in many different habitats supporting almost every species of savannah animal in South Africa. Although the area mostly comprises flat, gently undulating plains at an altitude of 250–400 m, these are occasionally broken by isolated hills (inselbergs or kopjes). The Lebombo Mountains manifest as a series of low hills in the eastern half of the park. To the north of Punda Maria, and in the extreme southwest, bedrock comprising granite, sandstone and quartzite outcrops form rugged hills.

Three different soil types overlie the rock formations: granitic soils dominate the western half of Kruger and basaltic soils the east, and a belt of sandy Karoo sediments separates them. Compounding its geological diversity is the fact that Kruger stretches through three degrees of latitude. This complexity gives rise to a series of different deciduous woodland and savannah ecotypes in 13 major habitat divisions or biomes (see map on *page 22*). However, for simplicity the habitats can be divided into three broad categories, as summarized below, and are recognized by certain characteristic plants (see *pages 18–21*):

Plains and open woodland Open grassland with scattered trees, such as Knobthorn, occurs on basaltic and Karoo soils, particularly in the southeastern parts of the park (*e.g.* Satara, Lower Sabie and Crocodile Bridge). The vegetation comprises many types of grasses, characteristic species including Red Grass, Digit Grass and Buffalo Grass.

Forest and riverine thickets Whilst large areas of continuous forest are absent in Kruger, there are stands of riparian thicket and forest-like woodland along the major rivers. Dominant and distinctive plants include Sycamore Fig, Fever Tree, Wild Date Palm, Sausage Tree and, in the south of the park, Weeping Boer-bean.

Broadleaved woodland A catch-all category for the woodland in Kruger that covers more than 65% of the park, though most extensive in the western half. Dominant plants include Sickle Bush, Silver Cluster-leaf and a variety of bushwillows. The central part of the park is dominated by Mopane, an abundant and distinctive tree that can be thinly spread throughout a grassy shrub savannah, but also occurs with Marula, bushwillows and fine-leaved thorn trees/shrubs, or can form dense, single-species woodland. The drier rugged northern region is typified by baobabs, which are common in the Limpopo River valley.

Broadleaved woodland dominates Kruger, comprising some 65% of the park.

Characteristic plants

Each of the three broad habitat types is characterized by particular plant species. These habitats, and in some cases particular plants, are mentioned throughout the species accounts – so familiarizing yourself with the habitat types, and learning a few plants will help you to focus your search for certain target animals. The purpose of this section is to illustrate these key plants, although it is worth bearing in mind that many trees lose their leaves in the dry season and will therefore look very different from the images shown here.

Plains and open woodland

The flat basalt plains and wooded grassland of eastern Kruger are excellent for grazers such as Plains Zebra, Common Wildebeest and African Buffalo.

Knobthorn *Senegalia nigrescens* occurs in dense thickets in broadleaved and open woodland, but also as scattered trees on open plains.

Digit Grass *Digitaria eriantha*

Red Grass
Themeda triandra

Buffalo Grass
Megathyrsus maximus

Forest and riverine thickets

Larger permanent and perennial rivers are flanked by forest and riverine thicket, sheltering Nyala, Bushbuck and Leopard.

Fever Tree *Vachellia xanthophloea* has unusual yellow bark.

Sycamore Fig *Ficus sycomorus*

Sausage Tree *Kigelia africana* has strange, sausage-shaped fruits.

Wild Date Palm *Phoenix reclinata*

Weeping Boer-bean *Schotia brachypetala* is most frequent in the southern half of the park.

Broadleaved woodland

The southern parts of the park are dominated by a variety of bushwillows, and the central and northern areas by Mopane (pictured here). These habitats are favoured by African Elephant and Giraffe.

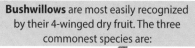

Bushwillows are most easily recognized by their 4-winged dry fruit. The three commonest species are:

Large-fruited Bushwillow
Combretum zeyheri

Silver Cluster-leaf *Terminalia sericea* is closely related to bushwillows and has a winged fruit.

Red Bushwillow *Combretum apiculatum*

Russet Bushwillow *Combretum hereroense*

Mopane *Colophospermum mopane* is the dominant tree of central and northern Kruger and has distinctive butterfly-shaped leaves.

Baobab *Adansonia digitata* is a giant, broad-trunked tree that is frequent in the northern parts of Kruger.

Sickle Bush *Dichrostachys cinerea* has a distinctive Chinese-lantern shaped flower.

Marula *Sclerocarya birrea* has distinctive fruits that are rich in vitamin C, popular with many fruit-eating animals; it is also used to make the famous cream liqueur Amarula.

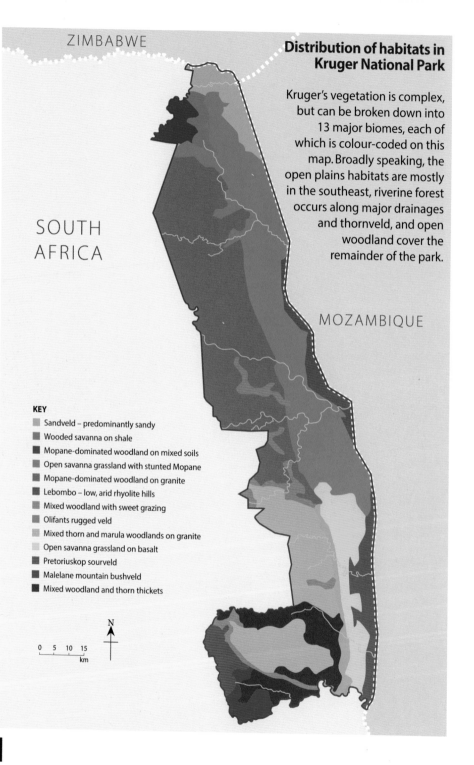

ZIMBABWE

Distribution of habitats in Kruger National Park

Kruger's vegetation is complex, but can be broken down into 13 major biomes, each of which is colour-coded on this map. Broadly speaking, the open plains habitats are mostly in the southeast, riverine forest occurs along major drainages and thornveld, and open woodland cover the remainder of the park.

SOUTH AFRICA

MOZAMBIQUE

KEY
- Sandveld – predominantly sandy
- Wooded savanna on shale
- Mopane-dominated woodland on mixed soils
- Open savanna grassland with stunted Mopane
- Mopane-dominated woodland on granite
- Lebombo – low, arid rhyolite hills
- Mixed woodland with sweet grazing
- Olifants rugged veld
- Mixed thorn and marula woodlands on granite
- Open savanna grassland on basalt
- Pretoriuskop sourveld
- Malelane mountain bushveld
- Mixed woodland and thorn thickets

N

0 5 10 15
km

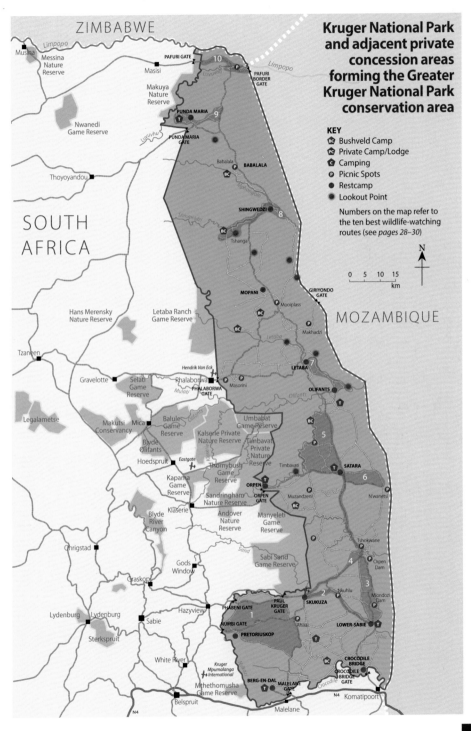

ZIMBABWE

Kruger National Park and adjacent private concession areas forming the Greater Kruger National Park conservation area

SOUTH AFRICA

MOZAMBIQUE

KEY
- BC Bushveld Camp
- PC Private Camp/Lodge
- C Camping
- P Picnic Spots
- ● Restcamp
- ✴ Lookout Point

Numbers on the map refer to the ten best wildlife-watching routes (see pages 28–30)

N

0 5 10 15
km

Limpopo

Musina
Messina Nature Reserve
Masisi
Makuya Nature Reserve
PAFURI GATE
PAFURI BORDER GATE
10
Limpopo
Luvuvhu

Nwanedi Game Reserve

PUNDA MARIA
PUNDA MARIA GATE
9

Thoyoyandou

Luvuvhu

Babalala
BABALALA
BC

SHINGWEDZI
BC
Tshanga
8

MOPANI
Mooiplaas
GIRIYONDO GATE

Hans Merensky Nature Reserve
Letaba Ranch Game Reserve
BC
Makhadzi
Letaba

Tzaneen

Gravelotte
Selati Game Reserve
Rhalaborwa
Hendrik Van Eck
PHALABORWA GATE
Masorini
LETABA
7
OLIFANTS
Olifants
Mulati

Legalametse
Makutsi Conservancy
Mica
Balule Game Reserve
Kalserie Private Nature Reserve
Umbabat Game Reserve
Timbavati Private Nature Reserve
BC
5
P
Blyde Olifants
Hoedspruit
Eastgate
Timbavati
SATARA
6

Kapama Game Reserve
Thornybush Game Reserve
ORPEN
ORPEN GATE
Muzandzeni
BC
N'wanetsi

Blyde River Canyon
Klaserie
Sandringham Nature Reserve
Andover Nature Reserve
Manyeleti Game Reserve
Tshokwane

Ohrigstad

Gods Window
Sabi Sand Game Reserve
4
Orpen Dam
3

Graskop

Lydenburg Lydenburg
Sabie
Hazyview
PHABENI GATE
PAUL KRUGER GATE
SKUKUZA
2
Nkuhlu
Mlondozi Dam

Sterkspruit
NUMBI GATE
PRETORIUSKOP
1
Afsaal
LOWER-SABIE

White River
Kruger Mpumalanga International
BC
CROCODILE BRIDGE
Mthethomusha Game Reserve
BERG-EN-DAL
MALELANE GATE
CROCODILE BRIDGE GATE
Crocodile

Belspruit
N4
Malelane
Komatipoort
N4

How, where and when to watch animals in Kruger National Park

Early to bed, early to rise

Camp and entrance gates have restrictions on when you are permitted to drive in the park (see table *below*), although some camp gates may open earlier (04h30) from November to January, so it is worth checking at your specific camp when you arrive. The best chance of seeing some of Kruger's most sought-after animals is within the first 30 minutes of the gates opening in the mornings. Staying out until the gate closing time is also an excellent strategy as nocturnal predators start to become active at dusk – though do not risk a hefty fine by missing the gate closing time! Resting up at midday is a good idea, particularly if you are doing night drives or walks, as your days will be pretty full.

Gates	Jan	Feb	Mar	Apr	May	Jun	Jul	Aug	Sep	Oct	Nov	Dec
Open	05h30		05h30	06h00		06h00		06h00		05h30	05h30	
Close	18h30		18h00	18h00		17h30		18h00		18h00	18h30	

Drive slowly, be vigilant

Do not be surprised if you see very little while cruising at the 50 km/h speed limit. Many of the most desired animals are masters of camouflage and driving at 25–30 km/h, and stopping regularly to scan, often reaps rewards. Look under the shade of trees, especially as the day warms up, and also stop at the waterholes and dams along your route.

Take an interest in all wildlife

Although many visitors come to Kruger to see the larger mammals, the smaller animals can be just as fascinating. On many occasions a stop to look at a chameleon, tortoise or bird can also reveal a big cat or other megafauna, so never neglect the smaller creatures. The birds in particular will always keep you entertained, so it is well worth getting the companion volume to this one by **WILD**Guides – *Birds of Kruger National Park*.

Waterholes and dams are always great places to visit, as animals need to drink regularly. With time and luck there is often some interesting behaviour to be seen.

Night drives in the park offer the best chance to observe some rarely seen nocturnal animals. It is also the time when the big cats are most active. Here a dominant male **Lion** is curling his lip back, performing what is known as the 'flehmen response', knowing that a pride female is ready to mate.

Go on the night drives and other park-scheduled activities

Most of the park camps now schedule night drives. If you are not solely obsessed with seeing the 'Big 5' this will be the best way of encountering the lesser-known nocturnal animals such as Springhares, genets, African Civets, jackals and much more. Of course, being out at night gives you a better chance of seeing larger predators actually doing something other than sleeping.

Get a map of the park

With a park the size of a small country you are going to need a map to navigate. The park shops sell maps that as well as being very useful for route planning, showing waterholes, picnic stops, dirt roads, rivers etc., also include invaluable snippets of information.

Use the bush telegraph

Sometimes the best information can be obtained by sharing news with other travellers. Your map will come in handy if directions from another traveller start getting complex! Although it can be a little annoying to be constantly flagged down and asked "What have you seen?", if you do have some information of your own, stopping someone to divulge it might just get you some other prize piece of information in return.

Use the sightings boards at the camps

Sightings boards at the camps get updated each day. Often the animals that are reported move on quickly, but if it is Lions on a carcass, or a Leopard up a tree, they may hang around and it is definitely worth a look. Also, these boards are great places to share information with other guests who may be gathered there.

Make a plan

Once you have gleaned any information that is available, make a plan for your day. Remember to consider places for comfort breaks, and also plan where you are going to get your meals. Keep snacks and water in the vehicle at all times, as you never know how long you will have to wait for a cat to wake up and walk out from under a bush.

If in doubt follow the river

Most animals need water, so if you are uncertain about where to go on your drive it makes sense to include several stops at waterholes or follow a river. If it is hot and quiet, then consider waiting at a dam or hide and you will be surprised what happens if you give it time.

Traffic jams are good

If you see a collection of vehicles, then it is a sure sign that something good has been seen. Although you are likely to be excited, it is important to be considerate in these situations. Unfortunately, with increasing visitation to the park has come an increase in impolite behaviour. The simple rule is to avoid parking directly in front of someone who has their binoculars up, and not to block the road or stop where it could leave others in a dangerous position. Be aware of other people trying to move through the traffic or departing from the sighting – making space for them will probably increase your chances of edging closer to a prime slot. It is important to pay attention when people begin to move their vehicles as there have been many collisions in these situations!

Bring binoculars and camera gear

If you want to make the most of your visit, remember to bring a decent pair of binoculars (preferably 8×32, or 10×42) and/or a camera. These days, point-and-shoot cameras are very good and will help you capture hundreds of fantastic memories of your safari. If you have an SLR, bring a 70–200 mm lens for most of the mammal photography, and at least a 300 mm lens for birds and smaller animals.

Picnic areas and other designated locations where you are allowed to leave your vehicle are great places to exchange information with other travellers, to stretch your legs or to have a 'sundowner'.

Always respect the animals

It is essential to remember that you are in the animal's domain, and that trifling with a buffalo, elephant or hippo could result in injury or worse. Always give animals space to move around and never feed them. Monkeys and baboons have become a serious problem at some of the picnic areas, where they are impulsive kleptomaniacs – even employing diversionary tactics to distract you while a collaborator steals your breakfast. Unfortunately, once they start hurting people, these animals will be eliminated by the park authorities. So leave them alone and do not feed them, otherwise you will be helping to consign them to their deaths.

Interpreting signs of the bush

When animals move through the bush they leave behind signs of their presence – tracks, scent and dung (spoor). Humans have a long history of using these clues when hunting animals, and our ancestors relied on this approach as a vital survival tool. It is unfortunate that in a modern world dominated by concrete and steel most of us have forgotten this art. However, looking for signs is still one of the best ways of finding mammals, and the illustrations of prints included in this book (see *pages 32–39*) should help you identify the animal responsible for leaving a particular track. Although these illustrations will be much easier to use on a walking safari, if you are on a dirt road and see a fresh large cat track imprinted over the last vehicle track, stop – the chances are that the animal is nearby. Wait and watch, as it might return. Animals often mark their territories with urine and dung, and a fresh midden or the strong smell of urine, are other useful signs to look out for. Similarly, vultures and eagles descending to the ground are a sure indication of a fresh carcass, and alarm calls sounded by monkeys, baboons or ungulates suggest that danger, often a predator, is nearby. Also, if the members of a large herd of ungulates are all looking in the same direction, they have probably noticed something that makes them uneasy.

This **Hippopotamus** may look placid when loafing in a pond, but it is important to be aware that this is their domain: respect their space and do not approach too close.

The ten best wildlife-watching routes

Just about any road can lead to a magical Kruger moment, but some routes regularly turn out to be better than others. The following are ten of the drives that are recommended by experienced visitors to the park. For ease of reference, the location and routing of each loop is annotated on the map on *page 23*.

1. Pretoriuskop loops

Pretoriuskop is an excellent camp; it is small and attracts relatively few visitors. The Fayi loop around the camp and the S7 and S3 roads heading north from Numbi gate all offer great local drives. This is one of the best places in the park to see **rhinos**, **African Wild Dog** and **Southern Reedbuck**, and **Side-striped Jackal** is regular on the night drives. It is definitely one of the better camps for those interested in seeing more than the 'Big 5'. If you have time on your hands, a drive down the historical Voortrekker Road to Afsaal (which serves great breakfasts), and then north on the H3 and back to Pretoriuskop on the H1-1 serves as a longer excursion with many rewards.

2. Skukuza to Lower Sabie

Following the Sabie River in an easterly direction from Skukuza (H1-1, which turns into the H4-1) can result in a sighting of almost any of Kruger's star animals, and it is a particularly reliable route for Leopard. The only drawback is that as it is one of the park's main roads, it can get very crowded. Near Skukuza, Lake Panic Hide on the S42 can be an excellent place to relax and look for smaller animals.

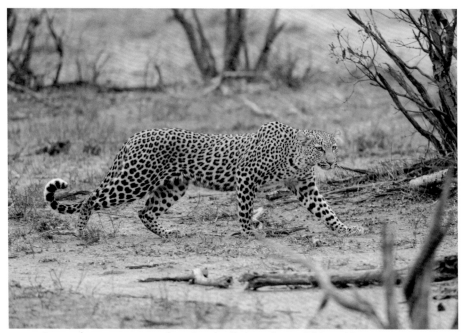

Leopards can appear anywhere, but the Skukuza, Lower Sabie and Satara areas are among the most reliable for this, the most secretive big cat.

3. Lower Sabie to Tshokwane

Close to Lower Sabie, Sunset Dam is a great location, especially for photography. The H10 that heads to Tshokwane is amazing for its variety of wildlife encounters. The 'Big 5', **Cheetah** and grazers, including large herds of **zebra** and **wildebeest** are all seen regularly. The S128 and S29 dirt roads and their waterholes are also well worth the diversion.

4. Skukuza to Satara

The H1-2 and H1-3 routes pass through probably some of the best bush for cats in the park and feature several waterholes, such as Mantimahle and Leeupan, that are good for **African Elephant** and grazers. The Satara region is a well-known **Lion** hotspot, but **Cheetah**, **Leopard** and **African Wild Dog** are also frequently encountered. Tshokwane is a great place to have a snack. If staying at Satara, be sure to take a night drive as this frequently produces **African Civet**, **White-tailed Mongoose**, **Serval**, **genets** and **galagos**.

5. Satara to Timbavati

Satara offers many options and is a favorite part of the park for many regular visitors. Consult the sightings boards for ideas, but one particularly good route is along the Timbavati Road. Take the H7 to the Nsemani Dam, where there is almost always something interesting happening. Head west a further 12 km to the junction with the S39 and turn north along the Timbavati Road. A stop at Leeubron is recommended for photographers because of the animal activity and frequently good lighting. Timbavati picnic area has some facilities, but does not sell food. Stops at Ratelpan hide and Palm Springs waterholes are recommended. Heading south the H1-4, back to Satara, passes through **Lion** country.

The southern third of the park is best for **White Rhinoceros**.

6. Satara-Nwanetsi loop

For good reason, the S100 Nwanetsi River Road just 2 km south of Satara is popular – the vegetation is open and 'big cat' sightings are regular. At the junction with the S41, head south to N'wanetsi viewpoint and Sweni hide, at both of which it is worth spending a little time. Drive back to Satara on the H6 for some variation.

7. Olifants to Letaba River roads

Olifants is a magical camp – situated on a hill with the river below, it has some of the most striking scenery in the park. The night drives here yield scarcer wildlife such as **Springhare** and **Sharpe's Grysbok**. The drive to Letaba along the S44, S90 and S46 is enchanting and provides good opportunities for encountering **Hippos** and **African Elephant**; it also offers probably your best chance of seeing an **otter** in the park. The hills are less favourable for **Lions** but better for **Leopards**.

Sharpe's Grysbok is best seen in the central portions of Kruger, particularly during night drives from Olifants Rest Camp.

8. Shingwedzi loops

As you head farther north, game sightings become less frequent, but there is an increased chance of seeing some of the rarer species. The main drive from Shingwedzi is down the S52, skirting the Nkayini riverbed, and the Gubyane waterhole and Tshange lookout are worthy diversions. Next to Shingwedzi is the amazing Kanniedood Dam, which has a resident **Leopard**, and is a draw for much of the region's wildlife including some of Kruger's rarest antelopes such as **Tsessebe**, **Sable Antelope** and, for the very lucky, **Roan Antelope**.

Tsessebe are found most reliably near Shingwedzi, along with some of Kruger's other rare antelopes.

9. Punda Maria

The Mahonie loop road that runs around the hills of Punda is stunning. This is a particularly good area for **Sharpe's Grysbok** and massive herds of **African Buffalo**. The drive to Klopperfontien Dam can also yield **Sable Antelope**.

10. Pafuri

There is no camp here and visitors either have to make a long day trip from Punda Maria, or stay outside the park. More for the connoisseur, or someone who has covered Kruger's south and central regions comprehensively, the river loops here are simply beautiful, and offer **Nyala** and excellent birdwatching opportunities.

Mammals

This section covers 57 of around 148 mammal species recorded in Kruger. Almost all of the predators, antelopes and large mammals are included. If you are interested in the park's small mammals, including the 75 or so species of shrews, bats and mice, you will need to refer to other sources of information (see *Further reading, page 170*).

Leopard

Mammal tracks

Animals often leave distinctive tracks (spoor) in soft ground. Working out what passed by your cabin during the night is a fun distraction in itself, and is likely to enhance your understanding of the bush. The tracks of the most frequently seen mammals are presented here alongside each other for comparative purposes. Each print is shown roughly to scale within its group. The average length (l) (*excluding claws unless indicated*) and, where useful, width (w) of a typical print are given for guidance, although it is worth remembering that prints can look larger on softer substrates such as sand. A scale bar is shown against each set of prints to provide an indication of size, and a ruler is printed on the inside back cover of the book to enable you to measure the actual size of any print you find.

Large prints

African Elephant (*p. 78*)

Hippopotamus (*p. 86*)

Black Rhino (*p. 84*)

White Rhino (*p. 82*)

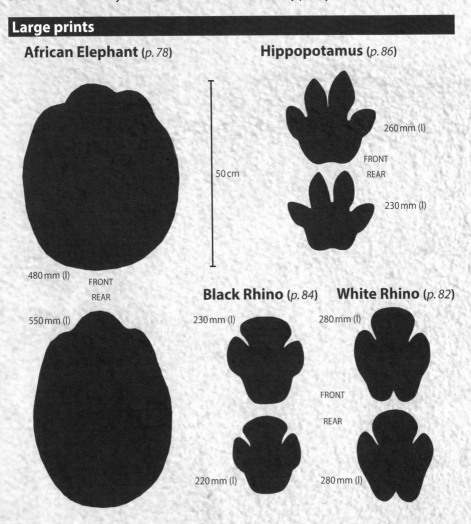

Strange prints

Scrub Hare
(*p. 128*)

35 mm (l)

FRONT

REAR

lengths include claws

40 mm (l)

Springhare
(*p. 129*)

40 mm (l)

lengths include claws

FRONT

REAR

50 mm (l)

10 cm

Cape Porcupine
(*p. 131*)

50 mm (l)

FRONT

REAR

80 mm (l)

Temminck's Ground Pangolin
(*p. 74*)

30 mm (l)

FRONT

REAR

60 mm (l)

Smith's Bush Squirrel (*p. 138*)

25 mm (l)

FRONT

REAR

45 mm (l)

Rock Hyrax
(*p. 130*)

40 mm (l)

FRONT

REAR

55 mm (l)

10 cm

Aardvark
(*p. 75*)

100 mm (l) including claws

FRONT

REAR

African Clawless Otter
(*p. 77*)

110 mm (l)

FRONT

REAR

120 mm (l)

Spotted-necked Otter
(*p. 76*)

85 mm (l)

FRONT

REAR

95 mm (l)

33

Dog-like prints

Spotted Hyena
(p. 58)

African Wild Dog
(p. 72)

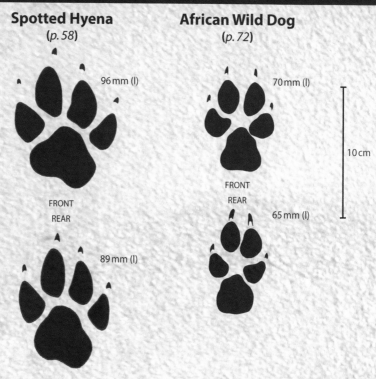

96 mm (l)

FRONT
REAR

89 mm (l)

70 mm (l)

FRONT
REAR

65 mm (l)

10 cm

Aardwolf *(p. 62)*

Black-backed Jackal
(p. 70)

Side-striped Jackal
(p. 71)

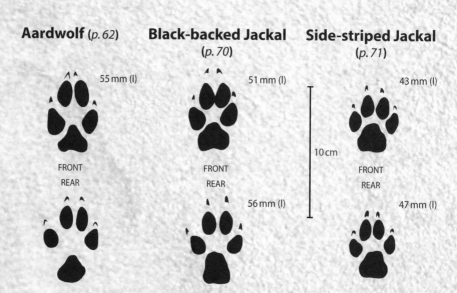

55 mm (l)

FRONT
REAR

51 mm (l)

FRONT
REAR

56 mm (l)

43 mm (l)

FRONT
REAR

47 mm (l)

10 cm

Cats

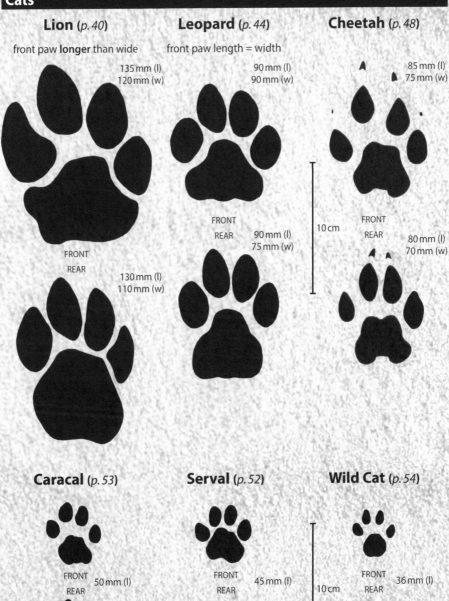

Lion (*p. 40*)

front paw **longer** than wide

135 mm (l)
120 mm (w)

FRONT

REAR

130 mm (l)
110 mm (w)

Leopard (*p. 44*)

front paw length = width

90 mm (l)
90 mm (w)

FRONT

REAR   90 mm (l)
75 mm (w)

Cheetah (*p. 48*)

85 mm (l)
75 mm (w)

10 cm

FRONT

REAR

80 mm (l)
70 mm (w)

Caracal (*p. 53*)

FRONT   50 mm (l)

REAR

Serval (*p. 52*)

FRONT   45 mm (l)

REAR

Wild Cat (*p. 54*)

10 cm

FRONT   36 mm (l)

REAR

African Civet *(p. 55)*

50 mm (l)
55 mm (w)

FRONT
REAR

FRONT
REAR

Common Genet *(p. 56)*

28 mm (l)

FRONT
REAR

Wild Cat for comparison

Large Spotted Genet *(p. 57)*

30 mm (l)

FRONT
REAR

10 cm

White-tailed Mongoose *(p. 67)*

41 mm (l)

FRONT
REAR

Side-striped Jackal for comparison

Jackal similar, but has larger toe impressions

Honey Badger *(p. 69)*

80 mm (l)

FRONT
REAR

75 mm (l)

10 cm

Zorilla *(p. 68)*

22 mm (l)

FRONT
REAR

Banded Mongoose (p. 64)

29 mm (l)

FRONT

REAR

Common Slender Mongoose (p. 66)

24 mm (l)

FRONT

REAR

Common Dwarf Mongoose (p. 65)

16 mm (l)

FRONT

REAR

10 cm

Primates

Vervet Monkey (p. 132)

80 mm (l)

HANDS

10 cm

100 mm (l)

FEET

Thick-tailed Greater Galago (p. 137)

40 mm (l)

HANDS

FEET

Southern Lesser Galago (p. 136)

30 mm (l)

HANDS

FEET

Chacma Baboon (p. 134)

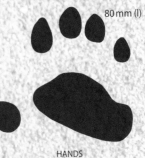

80 mm (l)

HANDS

150 mm (l)

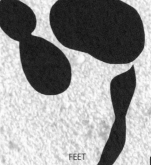

FEET

Cloven-hooved animals

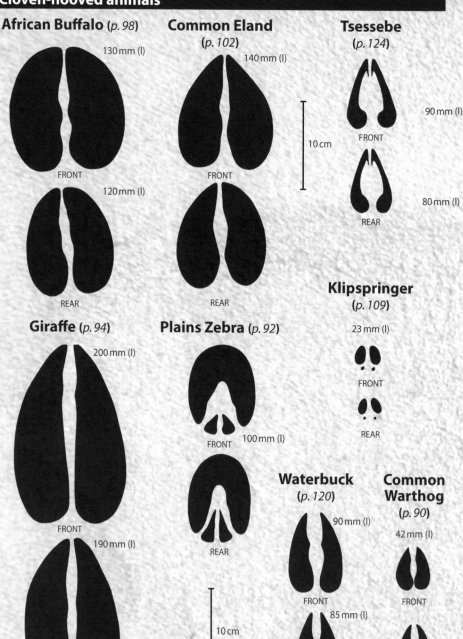

African Buffalo (*p. 98*)

130 mm (l)

FRONT

120 mm (l)

REAR

Common Eland (*p. 102*)

140 mm (l)

FRONT

REAR

10 cm

Tsessebe (*p. 124*)

90 mm (l)

FRONT

80 mm (l)

REAR

Giraffe (*p. 94*)

200 mm (l)

FRONT

190 mm (l)

REAR

Plains Zebra (*p. 92*)

FRONT

100 mm (l)

REAR

10 cm

Klipspringer (*p. 109*)

23 mm (l)

FRONT

REAR

Waterbuck (*p. 120*)

90 mm (l)

FRONT

85 mm (l)

REAR

Common Warthog (*p. 90*)

42 mm (l)

FRONT

REAR

Cloven-hooved animals

Nyala
(*p. 114*)

male
70 mm (l)

female
46 mm (l)

FRONT

REAR

Southern Reedbuck
(*p. 110*)

45 mm (l)

FRONT

REAR

Common Duiker
(*p. 106*)

35 mm (l)

FRONT

REAR

Bushbuck
(*p. 112*)

45 mm (l)

FRONT

10 cm

REAR

Greater Kudu
(*p. 104*)

male
90 mm (l)

female
65 mm (l)

FRONT

REAR

Impala
(*p. 122*)

50 mm (l)

FRONT

REAR

Sharpe's Grysbok
(*p. 107*)

25 mm (l)

FRONT

REAR

Steenbok
(*p. 108*)

37 mm (l)

FRONT

10 cm

REAR

Sable Antelope
(*p. 118*)

105 mm (l)

FRONT

90 mm (l)

REAR

Roan Antelope
(*p. 116*)

105 mm (l)

FRONT

REAR

Common Wildebeest
(*p. 126*)

100 mm (l)

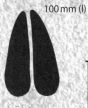

FRONT

10 cm

REAR

☐ **Lion** *Panthera leo*

Size: HB ♂ 172–250 cm, ♀ 158–192 cm; Tail 60–100 cm

Weight: ♂ 150–225 kg, ♀ 122–182 kg

Key identification features: Massive cat, uniform tawny-tan in colour. Youngsters have residual rosette-like spots that fade with age, although these are retained by some adults. The backs of the ears are black; muzzle and beard is pale blonde; tawny tail ends in a dark-tufted tip. Very rare 'white' colour morph occurs in Kruger, especially near Timbavati. Sexually dimorphic, mature males have a shaggy dark mane.

Habitat: Open and closed savannah, and riverine woodland. Prefers the zone between grassland and treed savannah.

Habits: Mostly active between dusk and dawn; lethargic during the day. Very sociable: prides consist of 4–6 mature females, a dominant (alpha) male or coalition of related males, and their cubs. Both sexes roar regularly to declare their territory, a sound that can carry 5 km.

Diet: Opportunistic generalists, the preferred prey is medium to large ungulates. Larger prides target larger prey, with certain individuals/prides specializing in particular species. Giraffe, Wildebeest and Zebra are the most frequent prey in Kruger.

The largest and most frequently encountered of the African cats. Lions are common and regularly seen in Kruger, although they are less frequent north of Shingwedzi.

Kruger is perfect Lion country, and the park is estimated to support around 1,700 individuals with an average pride size and

WHITE LIONS OF TIMBAVATI
The famous White Lions are not albinos, but are a result of a rare recessive colour gene. Discovered in the mid 1970s in the private Timbavati reserve adjacent to Kruger, three wild White Lions were taken to Pretoria Zoo for 'research' purposes and breeding. Wild White Lions seemingly died out, then in 2006 two cubs were born at Umbabat (near Timbavati). Other reintroduced White Lions have fared well, and although they remain exceedingly rare, are seen occasionally in the private reserves of the Timbavati area.

home range of 12 individuals and 25 km², respectively. Females form the stable nucleus of prides, while males, either alone or as a coalition of related individuals, tend to wander and attempt to take over any pride they encounter. After deposing the reigning males, they will remain with the females for as long as they can maintain the status quo. Their reign as top cat is relatively brief, normally 2–3 years, before stronger, younger upstarts replace them. New males typically kill any cubs from previous litters, thereby ensuring that only their genes are passed on to the next generation. Soon the females come into breeding condition and the pride will have new cubs sired by the reigning males. Once deposed, male coalitions stay together, but have to focus more on hunting as they can no longer rely on the females to do so for them.

The mane indicates male fitness and testosterone levels, and signals sexual dominance to the females, even at a great distance. Dominant males will mate-guard any females in breeding condition, seldom allowing females to stray more than a few metres from their side. Mating only lasts for about 60 seconds, but with bouts every 15–20 minutes over a period of 24–36 hours it can be quite exhausting. Females leave the pride to give birth in isolation and

One
of the
BIG 5

A male Lion in his prime

BIG CATS

The big cats of the genus *Panthera* appeared on Earth relatively recently, some 7–11 million years ago. Although Africa is now the world-famous big cat area, it is thought that the genus originated in Asia before spreading into Africa. Big cats are a massive draw for the millions of tourists that go on safari each year, with every encounter being an unforgettable highlight!

Lionesses are the main providers
of food for the pride.

return when the cubs are 4–8 weeks old. Occasionally several pregnant females in a pride will give birth at the same time. The resulting cubs are cared for communally, each cub suckling more than one female. However, cub mortality is high, with more than 50% dying in their first year. Sub-adult males are expelled from the pride when they are about three years old.

When hunting, prides often divide into smaller subgroups, each of which performs a different task. Working cooperatively in this way almost doubles their chances of making a successful kill. Larger females tend to fulfil the role of 'centre' and smaller females act as 'flanks'. They carefully stalk their intended prey to get as close as possible before making a rapid dash – at speeds of up to 60 km/h for a few hundred metres. The 'flanks' drive the prey towards the 'centre', which launches at the rump or shoulder and uses its retractile claws to anchor itself, and weight to bring down the prey, before suffocating the animal with a bite to the throat. If nearby, the pride males will partake of the meal, being afforded the honour of eating first.

THE MANE JOB

The main role of the dominant male is pride defence and ownership. They hunt infrequently, although can play a key role in subduing large prey. They often scavenge kills of other Lions or Spotted Hyenas. Battles between Spotted Hyenas and Lions are vicious and these two large social predators are constantly vying for local dominance. The victors are usually those that have the greater number, although Spotted Hyenas need to outnumber Lions by about 3:1 in order to be successful; the chances of Lions succeeding being greatly increased by the presence of a large male.

UNDER THREAT

Although Lions are frequently encountered in Kruger, the species is categorized as Vulnerable by the IUCN, having undergone a very significant population decline across Africa since the mid-1990s.

A seven-month-old cub: spotting on the legs is only lost when the animal is mature.

The mane on this young but fully-grown male is not
yet completely developed. He and his brothers will
have to hunt for themselves until they can take over
a pride from another male.

Leopard *Panthera pardus*

Size: HB ♂ 130–190 cm, ♀ 92–140 cm; Tail 60–110 cm

Weight: ♂ 35–90 kg, ♀ 28–60 kg

Key identification features: Large robust cat with black-and-brown rosettes on the blonde back and upper limbs, and solid black spots on the head, lower limbs and belly. Tail is marked above but whitish underneath. Cheetah (*page 48*) lacks rosettes and is much slimmer in build.

Habitat: Can be found almost anywhere, though in Kruger, it prefers thicker and rockier habitat, from which Lion and Spotted Hyena are absent, where it can remain out of sight during the day. Also hunts in riverbeds and riverine forest.

Habits: Primarily a nocturnal and crepuscular hunter, but also seen loafing in trees and dense cover and moves during the day. Solitary and elusive. Calls a rasping guttural "whuuu-huuuh" 5–10 times to proclaim its territory.

Diet: Prefers small and medium-sized mammals (mostly in the 8–40 kg range) and particularly Impala, but also takes birds, reptiles, fish and invertebrates.

This big cat is common and widespread in Kruger, with around 1,000 individuals in the park. Despite their number, Leopards are secretive and seen far less frequently than Lions or Spotted Hyenas. They are most often encountered at dawn, dusk, or on a night drive, and always a thrill to find.

Although superficially similar to the Cheetah, the Leopard is bulkier, lacks 'tear-marks' under the eyes and has mostly rosette-patterned spots, not solid ones. Leopards have extraordinarily long whiskers and sensitive hairs in their eyebrows that they use when navigating at night: these alert the cat to objects near to its face and sensitive eyes. The strong jaws and shoulder muscles enable Leopards to tackle large prey (although they typically prefer smaller prey). Their brute strength enables them to scale vertical tree trunks while carrying prey that weighs as much as themselves. They are extremely agile, can run at nearly 60 km/h, and leap up to 6 m forwards and 3 m into the air. Males have a home range of 30–78 km² and females 15–16 km², each home range overlapping with those of several members of the opposite sex. Both sexes will defend

their core territories vigorously against other Leopards of the same sex and use scent-marking, scratching with claws, and vocalizing to signal their territories. Fights resulting from territorial transgression can result in severe injury or death.

Individuals travel considerable distances each night when hunting, moving through the territories of other Leopards of the opposite sex. They pair briefly to mate, the female then returning to her core range to raise the cubs alone. After suckling for 70 days, cubs begin to take meat and venture out with their mother. Initially, they are very vulnerable and many are killed by other predators. By two years old they are able to hunt independently and are banished by their mothers. They then either establish their own territories or are killed in territorial battles.

Leopards hunt by stalking and pouncing, using their incredible camouflage to good effect when approaching prey in thickets. Chases are short, typically less than 30 m. The victim is killed by sheer force or, in the case of larger prey, suffocation. Leopards have retractable claws, and these are extended during the kill. The large 'dewclaw', a long claw located a few centimetres above the foot pad, helps to pin the prey down. Prey is often disembowelled. In Kruger, 31 prey species have been recorded, with Impala making up around 75% of the diet. Adult Leopards need about 10 kg of food every three days, but when they have cubs, or when prey is smaller, have to make kills more frequently. Kills are often stashed up a tree, or hidden in an inaccessible place, to avoid being lost to Lions or Spotted Hyenas. In times of abundance or opportunity, Leopards may kill more than they need and store prey for later consumption. Leopards prefer to rest up in caves or thickets, or on the thick limbs of trees, particularly if the tree is being used to store prey.

LEOPARDS AND BABOONS

Leopards will occasionally predate baboons. They prefer hunting stragglers on the edge of a troop, because venturing into the centre risks being attacked by many individuals. Large male baboons, in particular, have massive teeth and are more than capable of inflicting damage. Baboons have been known to turn the tables on Leopards: in one incident a troop was reported to have driven a Leopard up a tree, and then prevented it from descending for many hours. Eventually the baboons lost interest and moved on.

Leopards are secretive and seldom seen. Despite being common in Kruger they are categorized as Near Threatened by the IUCN, as they are declining outside large parks throughout Africa. The cut above the shoulder of this Leopard is either the result of a territorial scuffle with another Leopard or a puncture wound sustained when hunting.

☐ **Cheetah** *Acinonyx jubatus*

Size: HB 110–150 cm; Tail 65–90 cm

Weight: ♂ 39–59 kg, ♀ 36–48 kg

Key identification features: Tall and lithe, with black spots (not rosettes) all over tawny coat. Diagnostic black 'tear-marks' run from eyes to upper lip. At a distance the deep chest, concave back and narrow waist give it a distinctive appearance and gait. End of tail is black-banded and has a white tip.

Habitat: Grassy plains and woodland, including dense scrub.

Habits: Both diurnal and nocturnal, with activity peaking in early morning and late afternoon. No fixed social structure. Males are either solitary or form coalitions, typically with related males, and tend to be territorial. Females are solitary or in small family units with cubs, and roam widely through a home range that overlaps with several male territories. Some individuals may be semi-nomadic.

Diet: Specializes in small- and medium-sized antelope weighing less than 40 kg, especially young animals.

The Cheetah is the smallest of Africa's 'big cats' and is built like a greyhound. It is rare and seldom seen, with fewer than 200 individuals in Kruger, but can be encountered throughout the day. Although it may be confused with the Leopard, the Cheetah is slender, has 'tear-marks' under the eyes and solid spots, not rosette-patterned ones.

Almost every physical aspect of this cat is an adaptation to a life built for speed and manoeuvrability. The long, powerful limbs and waif-like body, combined with a flexible spine that increases stride length, makes this the fastest mammal on Earth. Cheetahs can accelerate from 0 to 90 km/h in six seconds (equalling some sports cars) and reach top speeds of 100 km/h. Cheetah's feet are unlike those of other cats – the claws are not retractable and function like a sprinter's spikes to give increased traction. They also have modified footpads that act as a high-speed braking and anti-skidding device. The tail is laterally

flattened and is used as a rudder to maintain balance and help the animal change direction at high speed. The animal's internal organs are also modified: an enlarged heart and adrenal glands help it to run faster during the chase, and enlarged lungs and nasal cavities increase air intake both during the hunt and also when the Cheetah is recovering after it has subdued its prey.

Cheetahs are primarily visual hunters and stalk their prey by hunching down and moving slowly until they are within striking distance. Chases seldom last more than a few hundred metres. In a groundbreaking study published in the prestigious scientific journal *Nature*, zoologists recently showed that Cheetahs hunt both during the day and night, and that they were more successful when running through thick cover than

in the open. These findings contradict conventional wisdom and show how much we still have to learn about some of Africa's most charismatic animals. Another observation from this study was that that Cheetahs seldom hunted at top speed: it seems that they need to run slower to retain maximum manoeuvrability and enable them to catch darting prey such as Impalas. Powerful muscles enable the cat to accelerate and decelerate by 15 km/h in a single stride, allowing it to change direction very quickly. Cheetahs normally trip their prey, or slap it down using the 'dewclaw', a long claw located a few centimetres above the foot pad. Prey is often suffocated once subdued, and moved to cover. Cheetahs often lose their prey to larger predators, and once it is felled have limited time to eat their quarry. As a result, they often gorge themselves and can eat 15 kg of meat in 20–30 minutes, usually starting on the highly nutritious hindquarters.

Cheetahs differ from Leopards by having a deeper chest, arched back, 'tear-marks' and solid spots.

Cheetahs are either loners or occur in small groups. In parks elsewhere in Africa they follow migratory game and are semi-nomadic, but in Kruger they tend to be territorial, occupying small home ranges of about 175 km^2. Receptive females will allow a suitor to approach her, and this is generally the only time that she will associate with another adult. However, she may mate with many males over the several days that she is receptive. After mating, she goes her own way, giving birth to 3–5 (rarely more) downy cubs after 90 days. Cub mortality is high, and they are frequently killed by other predators and even baboons. The mother teaches her cubs to hunt and after 15–20 months they go their own way.

KRUGER'S MOST THREATENED CAT
The Cheetah, the rarest of Kruger's big cats, is also globally threatened and classified as Vulnerable by the IUCN. The estimate of 120–200 individuals for Kruger makes this the most significant population in South Africa.

KING CHEETAH AND GENETICS

There have been several records of King Cheetah in Kruger, a very rare colour morph caused by a recessive gene. They are much darker with broad black stripes running down their back and a darker, blotchy (not spotted) pattern on their sides and flanks. It is hypothesized that Cheetah numbers plummeted to just a few hundred individuals during the last ice age, and it very nearly died out. The resultant genetic 'bottleneck' and inbreeding means that genetic variability in Cheetahs is extremely low. This has had a negative impact on sperm structure and breeding success, an increased susceptibility to disease, and possibly led to the occurrence of the King Cheetah recessive gene.

King Cheetahs, like this individual, are mostly seen in captivity but are occasionally found in the park: seeing one would undoubtedly be a red-letter day!

☐ Serval *Leptailurus serval*

Size: HB 59–92 cm; Tail 20–38 cm

Weight: ♂ 9–13·5 kg, ♀ 7–12 kg

Key identification features: Tall, slender cat with short tail and disproportionately small head with large, oval ears. The back of the ears have bold white 'eye' patches. Tawny-coloured with dense black blotching that sometimes forms stripes on the shoulders and neck.

Habitat: Tall grass, thickets or reedbeds close to permanent water.

Habits: Nocturnal and crepuscular, though diurnal activity is also recorded. Solitary. Territorial with small home range of approximately 10 km².

Diet: Small mammals, especially rodents weighing 200 g or less, as well as birds, larger mammals, reptiles and invertebrates.

This medium-sized cat is uncommon in Kruger. Its nocturnal and secretive habits mean that it is not frequently seen, and your best chance of encountering one is on a night drive. Its size, combined with long legs and large oval ears make it almost unmistakable. Servals have very sensitive hearing and a unique hunting style. This involves standing quietly in tall cover, for up to 15 minutes, listening for potential prey and then pouncing a considerable distance (3–6 m horizontally and over 1–2 m vertically) to strike. Prey is also hooked out of burrows using mobile toes and long claws.

The sexes only associate during breeding. After an 80-day gestation, two kittens are born in a den. They start hunting at six months and remain with the mother for 12 months before being expelled.

☐ **Caracal** *Caracal caracal*

Size: HB 61–105 cm; Tail 20–34 cm

Weight: ♂ 8–20 kg, ♀ 6·2–16 kg

Key identification features: Unspotted cat; sandy-brown to brick-red in colour; powerful hind-quarters taller than the shoulders; short tail. Muzzle, chin and eye-sockets white, contrasting with black lips, nose, and mid-forehead stripe. Has unique wispy black tufts off the back of the black ears.

Habitat: Varied savannah.

Habits: Nocturnal and crepuscular. Solitary. Territorial against same-sex individuals, but ranges overlap with territories of opposite sex.

Diet: Small to medium mammals weighing 5 kg or less; less frequently birds. Seldom takes carrion.

Uncommon in Kruger, this medium-sized cat is nocturnal and secretive and the best chance of encountering one is on a night drive. The Caracal's size, red coat and pointed ears make it almost unmistakable. They stalk small mammals before pouncing from about 5 m, and catch birds by leaping with powerful hind legs. Excess prey is cached to be fed on later.

Mating takes place over a 4–6-day period. Some females copulate with different males, possibly according to some kind of 'pecking order', whereas others are guarded by a male who fends off rivals. After 75 days, 1–6 kittens are born in a shelter; they join their mother on hunting forays after two months.

The Caracal is the only cat in Kruger with pointed ears and wispy ear tufts.

Size: HB 46–67 cm; Tail 25–36 cm	
Weight: ♂ 4·0–6·2 kg, ♀ 2·4–5·0 kg	
Key identification features: Similar to the domestic cat, but separated by tawny-red hind ear coloration and longer, more slender legs. Coloration variably grey-brown; tail dark-tipped.	
Habitat: Almost anywhere with cover.	
Habits: Nocturnal. Terrestrial, but can climb trees. Solitary. Territorial against same-sex individuals, but ranges overlap with territories of opposite sex.	
Diet: Small mammals, particularly mice and rats, as well as birds, reptiles and invertebrates.	

This small cat resembles a 'tabby cat' and, although common, is elusive and seen infrequently in Kruger, usually on night drives. As the only small 'wild' cat, it is not easily confused with any of Kruger's other cats. It hunts by stealthily approaching prey and pouncing from about 1m. Males (sometimes several) will mate-guard receptive females, before mating and then departing. Some 60 days later, 2–5 kittens are born in a hole or burrow. The young require maternal care for several months before venturing on hunting forays, and after reaching sexual maturity at six months are chased from the mother's territory.

Wild Cats are distributed widely across Eurasia and Africa, the 'African' subspecies becoming distinct about 130,000 years ago. The species was domesticated in the Middle East as recently as 10,000 years ago, and hybridization between domestic and 'wild' individuals is frequent. However, the animals in Kruger are truly wild.

■ African Civet *Civettictis civetta*

Size: HB 67–84 cm; Tail 34–47 cm	

Weight: 7–20 kg (♀ heavier than ♂)

Key identification features: Stocky, long-bodied and squat. More bull-necked with a much shorter black-tipped tail than genets (*pages 56–57*). Hind legs, front legs and chest diagnostically black. The raccoon-like black mask lacks white splashes under the eyes (a feature of the genets).

Habitat: Prefers riverine forest and thick savannah.

Habits: Nocturnal and crepuscular. Solitary. Terrestrial, poor climbers, but will walk along branches to reach fruits.

Diet: Adaptable and variable, including small vertebrates, invertebrates, eggs and fruits. Diet varies seasonally.

This medium-sized relative of the genets looks more like a short-legged dog. It is fairly common in Kruger and frequently seen on night drives. The African Civet has the strongest jaw of any member of its family, but has compact feet that are unsuitable for climbing or digging. They apparently detect prey using their excellent sense of smell, and kill by biting rather than using their paws. Territories are demarcated by depositing faeces in middens called civitries, and by scent-marking using highly aromatic 'musk-like' glands. While these secretions are still used in perfumery, the development of synthetic 'musk' seems to have reduced the demand. If threatened, the hair on the back is raised to form a formidable crest, doubling the apparent size of the animal. The female can produce three litters a year and will only tolerate the male for the six days she is in oestrus. After 70 days, 1–4 cubs are born in a den. Cubs are weaned and accompany the mother after 60 days.

GENETS

Genets differ from civets in their more slender, sleek and almost serpentine shape, long, ringed tail and more pointed snout. Their fur is greyish-brown with dark spots, and white and dark smudges on the muzzle. Both genet species have variable-sized spots, making this an unreliable character for identification. The nature of the dorsal stripe and colour of the tail tip are the best identification features.

Genets are fairly common and frequently seen on night drives in Kruger. During the daytime, they use tree holes or Aardvark or Springhare burrows for shelter and to avoid predation. They prefer to forage on the ground, but will also climb trees when hunting. Genets move rapidly, trotting along with body and head held low to the ground. They have a well developed sense of smell that is often used to locate prey, which they either stalk or rush in and bite or claw randomly to kill. When feeding Genets are less discerning than other small predators, often swallowing feathers and bones.

Genets use large scent glands to mark their territory and produce a musky secretion when threatened. After mating and a gestation of 10–11 weeks, 2–5 kits are born in a den during the wet season when insects are most abundant. Cubs are weaned after nine weeks and join their mother on nocturnal foraging sorties.

◼ **Common Genet** *Genetta genetta*

Size: HB 46–52 cm; Tail 40–51 cm	**Habitat:** Savannah, preferring open woodland and dry grassland.
Weight: 1·8–2·6 kg	
Key identification features: Differs from similar Large-spotted Genet by having erectile hairs in the dark dorsal stripe that can be raised as a crest, and typically smaller, more uniform dark spots and a banded, white-tipped tail.	**Habits:** Nocturnal. Solitary. Secretive. Primarily terrestrial, but good climbers.
	Diet: Insects, mice, spiders, and sometimes birds, reptiles, frogs, other animals, and occasionally fruits.

Large-spotted Genet *Genetta maculata*

Size: HB 41–52 cm; Tail 39–54 cm

Weight: 1·4–3·2 kg

Key identification features: Although a dark dorsal line is present, it lacks the erectile hairs or dorsal crest found in Common Genet. Spots typically larger than in that species and with rusty centres, and a banded, black-tipped tail.

Habitat: Prefers riverine forest and wetter woodland.

Habits: Nocturnal. Solitary. Secretive. Primarily terrestrial, but are good climbers.

Diet: Same as Common Genet.

HYENAS

The hyena genus *Crocuta* was widespread in Eurasia several million years ago, and dispersed to Africa before dying out in Eurasia. Scientists believe that hyenas were originally quite solitary creatures in the forested parts of Eurasia, and that the nature of the open savannahs in Africa, and intense competition from other predators at carcasses, may have resulted in Spotted Hyenas becoming social animals.

☐ Spotted Hyena *Crocuta crocuta*

Size: HB 125–160 cm; Tail 22–27 cm

Weight: 45–86 kg (♀ heavier than ♂)

Key identification features: Stocky; broad, bull terrier-like head with large, rounded ears; back slopes characteristically from the shoulders to lower, rounded hindquarters. The pelt is grey-brown with varying darker spots and a pale fluffy crest running down the head and back. Young are very dark brown and lack spots.

Habitat: Savannah and thickets.

Habits: The most social carnivore. Clans can be large, females rule, and nepotism is the norm, with daughters of dominant (alpha) females outranking other females. Communal dens are used.

Diet: Highly opportunistic, preferring medium and large ungulates like Impala in Kruger. They kill about 75% of their food, scavenging the remainder.

BRAINS OR BRAWN
Hyenas are brutes, but they are also surprisingly intelligent with a well-developed brain. They can even outperform Chimpanzees in certain problem-solving tests.

The Spotted Hyena is a large, gregarious, dog-like animal. It is common and widespread in Kruger and, with over 4,000 individuals, is the park's most abundant large predator. It is hard to confuse, being much larger than the jackals, and less colourful than the African Wild Dog.

Territories are advertised by loud "*whoooop*" calls at night, and demarcated by a smelly white secretion, produced by large anal glands, that is smeared onto grass stalks. Hyenas will respect other clans' boundaries, reportedly curtailing a chase when quarry enters another clan's territory. Despite having a reputation for being a scrounger and a thief, this highly successful predator kills more often than it scavenges. Instead of stealth, Spotted Hyenas rely on endurance and stamina to tire their prey. Physiological adaptations for such chases include having a large heart (in relative terms double the size of a Lion's). Hyenas will disembowel or tear at their prey until it collapses. Endowed with jaws capable of exerting a force of $800\,kgf/cm^2$, and with teeth adapted for crushing, Spotted Hyenas can even consume the skin and bone of large animals.

Reproduction in Spotted Hyenas is bizarre. Females lack a typical vagina and instead have a pseudo-penis that is often larger than the male's penis. Mating and birth occur via an opening in the pseudo-penis, successful mating requiring careful positioning of the genitals. Mating takes place throughout the year and involves the dominant female of a clan and several males. No pair bonds are formed: instead, females favour males with which they have a pre-existing 'friendly' relationship, are

new to the clan, or are passive. Gestation lasts four months and giving birth can be complicated, the pseudo-penis often being ruptured in the process, taking weeks to heal. The well-developed cubs immediately begin attacking each other with their razor-sharp teeth to establish social dominance, about 25% being killed as a result. The milk of higher-ranking females contains high levels of male sex hormones (androgen); this makes their pups more masculine and better able to dominate the pups of lower ranking females.

The social dynamics of Spotted Hyenas are complex, appearing more similar to those of primates than to other carnivores. Relationships are key, with dominance determined by size and aggression, as well as by the network of relationships they form with other high-ranking hyenas (*e.g.* males will appease higher-ranking

HYENA BODY LANGUAGE
Hyenas have complex body language: ears flat with teeth bared is a sign of fear; lowered hindquarters indicates retreating from attack; erect tail is a sign of aggression; and walking on fore-knees shows submission.

females in order to elevate their own status). Females are larger than males and dominate the clans in a matriarchal society. Clan members compete as much as they cooperate, with access to kills and mating opportunities all being determined by social status. Unlike some social predators, females never care for the pups of other females, and males exhibit little paternal care. Female dominance is not well understood, but it is believed to increase a female's access to kills and thus ensure milk production for her cubs. Females remain with their birth clans, although males leave after 2–3 years.

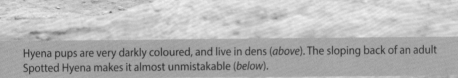

Hyena pups are very darkly coloured, and live in dens (*above*). The sloping back of an adult Spotted Hyena makes it almost unmistakable (*below*).

☐ **Aardwolf** *Proteles cristata*

Size: HB 55–80 cm; Tail 20–30 cm

Weight: 8–12 kg

Key identification features: Small, dainty relative of hyenas, the size of a jackal. Silver-gold coat has widely spaced vertical black tiger-like stripes and the muzzle, feet and tail are black.

Habitat: Grassy fringes of pans, open grassland.

Habits: Nocturnal, spending the day in underground burrows. Pairs (sometimes with offspring) will forage separately each night; they do not associate outside the breeding season.

Diet: Insects, especially termites.

Aardwolves are small, dog-like relatives of the hyenas. Once regular in southern Kruger, they are now extremely rare, perhaps even locally extinct. The name in Afrikaans translates as 'Earth Wolf' and is derived from their propensity to spend the day in burrows underground. Although capable of digging their own burrows, they prefer to use abandoned Aardvark, Cape Porcupine or Springhare burrows.

Although superficially similar to hyenas, having a sloping back, an extended muzzle, and anal glands, Aardwolves are actually quite different, being strictly insectivorous with a very strong preference for termites. Adaptations for this diet include a long spatula-shaped tongue covered in very sticky saliva for enmeshing hapless prey, and reduced peg-like teeth for crunching insects. The long canines have been retained for territorial defence.

Aardwolves are tolerant of the terpene-like chemicals that termites use to fend off attack from other predators. Because their prey is so small, Aardwolves may need to forage for 6–7 hours each night to consume the 300,000 termites (2 kg) that they need to survive. Aardwolves detect termites using a combination of scent and sound, using their large ears to pick up the movements in the colony. They also rely on memory, revisiting previously productive mounds at regular intervals. Unlike Aardvarks (*page 75*), they do not dig into and destroy the mounds, instead licking their prey off the surface.

Pairs occupy approximately 4 km² territories that they defend against intruders by raising their manes to exaggerate their size. Territories are marked using musky secretions from the anal gland. Once a territory has been established, the pair is socially monogamous for the breeding season, but extra-pair copulations may be as high as 40%.

After a three-month gestation, 1–4 pups are born. They remain hidden in the den until they are six weeks old, and thereafter emerge regularly to play above ground. They suckle during their first four months and then join their parents foraging for termites. Both parents care for the young, protecting them from attacks by predators. Pups mature quickly and are independent by seven months; they are usually expelled from the territory just before they are a year old.

AARDWOLF HISTORY

Although the Aardwolf resembles a dog, it diverged from cat-like ancestors such as civets (*page 55*) and mongooses (*pages 65–67*) some 25 Million Years Ago (MYA). These primitive 'hyenas' were initially small animals, eating insects, birds and small mammals. Then, between 15–11 MYA, the family diversified into two groups each containing several species: dog-like hyenas; and bone-crushing hyenas. The Aardwolf is the last remaining member of the dog-like hyenas, with all its cousins having died out. Competition from dominant dog-like predators (*e.g.* jackals) probably forced modern 'hyenas' to become specialists in food sources such as termites or carrion.

Once quite a regular sight in Kruger, the Aardwolf is now extremely rare in the park. The reasons for this change in abundance are uncertain, but may be related to the way in which fire management has affected its termite and ant food source.

☐ Banded Mongoose *Mungos mungo*

Size: HB 30–40 cm; Tail 17–31 cm

Weight: 0·9–1·9 kg

Key identification features: Sturdy, medium-sized mongoose. Fur is greyish-brown with 11–13 obvious dark transverse bands extending from the mid-back to the tail base. Huge group size.

Habitat: Woodland with suitable cover.

Habits: Diurnal. Colonial and gregarious in groups of 7–30. Shelters communally in dens (*e.g.* in abandoned termite mound). Terrestrial, but will forage in trees.

Diet: Invertebrates, especially beetles and millipedes. Sometimes vertebrates.

Banded Mongooses are very sociable animals.

A large, and gregarious mongoose that is common throughout Kruger. Told from other mongooses by its large size and bands running over the back. Groups of Banded Mongoose den together each night, favouring large termitaria with many entrances. However, if no den is available they huddle together on the ground or under a bush. Large groups forage together in a loose association, with each individual searching for its own food. Prey (including grubs below ground) are located by smell and dug up using their long claws.

There is no strict social hierarchy, but older females tend to dominate and copulate with 1–3 dominant males. Colony females synchronize births, often to the day, producing large communal litters. After a month the pups emerge from the den, each forming an association with a helper that will be its exclusive escort, protector and provider until independence. When groups get too large, young females and subordinate males are expelled. Inter-group rivalries are intense and fighting is frequent. The standard response towards predators is to rear-up on the hind legs and stand upright; if that fails to deter the predator, then the mongooses scatter at high speed to the nearest refuge.

☐ Common Dwarf Mongoose *Helogale parvula*

Size: HB 16–23 cm; Tail 14–19 cm

Weight: 213–341 g

Key identification features: Smallest mongoose, with short and thin tail. Smooth coat is uniformly dark brown. Grizzled greyish face.

Habitat: Woodland with undergrowth.

Habits: Diurnal. Colonial and gregarious in groups of 2–20. Alpha pair dominates colony, assisted by helpers. Uses dens for shelter. Terrestrial, but will forage in trees.

Diet: Invertebrates, especially beetles and termites, but also millipedes, larvae, small vertebrates, and seeds.

This small, group-living mongoose is common throughout Kruger and told from other mongooses by its tiny size and dark brown coloration. It is Africa's smallest carnivore and favours termitaria for use

TOOL-USERS
Common Dwarf Mongooses sometimes gain access to the contents of a bird's egg by cracking it against a rock until the shell breaks.

as communal dens. Loose groups forage each morning and evening and rest in the midday heat. The dominant (alpha) female is most frequently the eldest and favours the alpha male, although both will mate with other lower-ranked individuals. The result is a hierarchy that heavily favours the alpha pair, with 70% of the offspring being theirs. Subdominant adults are suppressed both hormonally and behaviourally and the survival rate of non-alpha pups is low. The entire group cooperates in raising the pups; lactating 'baby-sitters' remain at the den and act as wet nurses while the remainder of the colony forages. Once weaned, pups are adopted by a mentor that provides food, grooming, and protection.

☐ Common Slender Mongoose *Herpestes sanguineus*

Size: HB 27–34 cm; Tail 23–30 cm

Weight: ♂ 523–789 g, ♀ 373–565 g

Key identification features: Small, short-legged and daintily built. Long, gently curving tail with a characteristically tufted black tip. Body colour variable grey to red-brown.

Habitat: Catholic, preferring hollow logs and rocky shelter.

Habits: Primarily diurnal. Mostly solitary. Not strongly territorial, but male coalitions or females with offspring will have a home range. Adept at climbing trees, they are still primarily terrestrial.

Diet: Varies seasonally, with insects (especially grasshoppers) preferred in the wet season. Also eats other invertebrates, lizards, rodents, snakes, birds, amphibians, carrion and fruits.

The black tail-tip is distinctive.

This medium-sized mongoose is widespread but uncommon in Kruger; it is told from other mongooses by its elongated body and long, black-tipped tail. They often forage along grassland edges, darting in and out of cover, and are frequently taken by birds of prey. When disturbed, they freeze or rear up on their hind legs.

Surprisingly, Common Slender Mongooses sometimes den with other species of mongoose. Males have territories that overlap with those of several females, and are attracted to sexually receptive females by the scent they emit. The 1–3 young are born in a concealed hollow late in the wet season when insects are abundant, males playing no role in parental care.

◼ White-tailed Mongoose *Ichneumia albicauda*

Size: HB 47–69 cm; Tail 34–49 cm
Weight: 2·9–5·2 kg
Key identification features: Large, long-legged and tall mongoose. Head is elongated and tapering. Body fur is grizzled brown, silver and grey. Legs black. Tail long, bushy and white.
Habitat: Savannah and riverine forest.
Habits: Mostly nocturnal; most active early in the evening and on darker nights. Mainly solitary, occasionally in pairs or small female clans. Terrestrial.
Diet: Primarily insects, but also vertebrates, scorpions, spiders, berries and fruits. Ants and termites in the dry season, dung beetles in the wet season.

A large, solitary, nocturnal mongoose that is uncommon but widespread in Kruger. It is told from other mongooses by its large, bushy, white tail, and by the fact that it is primarily active at night. Its structure is more dog-like than other mongooses and it has a trotting-gait, with head slung low and the heavy hind-quarters giving the back a forward-sloping posture. When foraging it can travel over 4 km in an hour.

Despite being accomplished diggers, White-tailed Mongooses do not excavate their own burrows, instead spending the day holed-up in a crevice, termite mound, Aardvark burrow or other cavity. The sexes have overlapping territories and females may form clans. Scent from a conspicuous anal pouch, urine and dung are used for territorial marking. Mating only lasts for a few hours and the resulting litter size is 1–4; the females rear their young alone.

(Striped Polecat)

The Zorilla is a distinctive small, nocturnal skunk-like carnivore in the weasel family. It occurs throughout Kruger but is scarce and rarely seen, even on night drives. It has a small stomach which means it must eat frequently and therefore spends much of its time foraging, detecting prey by sight or smell. Zorillas have a varied diet: they dig for prey in loose soil or leaf-litter, track larger mammals into their burrow, kill snakes and other reptiles by bites to the back, neck and/or head, and also eat birds' eggs. They are aggressive and if threatened warn off potential predators by arching their back and aiming their rear-end at the opponent, in a similar manner to a skunk. Failure to retreat will result in the ejection of a noxious 'tear-gas'-like fluid which may temporarily blind the aggressor or irritate its mucous membranes. They are generally solitary, only associating with others when breeding, and use faeces and pungent anal emissions as territorial markers. Gestation is 36 days and 2–3 kits are born in an underground nest.

Size: HB 28–38 cm; Tail 17–28 cm

Weight: ♂ 0·8–1·2 kg, ♀ 0·4–0·75 kg

Key identification features: Skunk-like, with black and white stripes. Larger size, three white facial patches, and a mixture of black and white hair on tail distinguish it from the **African Weasel** *Poecilogale albinucha* (rare in Kruger; not illustrated).

Habitat: Widespread in woodland, grassland and riverine forest.

Habits: Nocturnal. Rests in burrows, crevices and log hollows during the day. Terrestrial, but able to climb and swim well. Solitary, except during mating.

Diet: Insects, spiders, other invertebrates, small mammals, birds, and other vertebrates.

☐ Honey Badger *Mellivora capensis*
(Ratel)

Size: HB 73–96 cm; Tail 20–29 cm

Weight: ♂ 7·7–14·6 kg, ♀ 6·2–13·6 kg

Key identification features: Stocky, thickset with a short tail. Ears tiny. Distinctly pied, with a whitish-grey saddle contrasting with a black lower half, creating a capped appearance.

Habitat: Almost anywhere in Kruger.

Habits: Primarily nocturnal. Generally solitary; pairs when breeding. Mostly terrestrial, but can climb trees.

Diet: Famous for molesting bee hives and eating honey, but mostly eats mice, spiders, scorpions, lizards, insects, millipedes, birds, snakes and even vegetation.

Although uncommon and seldom seen in Kruger, the Honey Badger's contrasting pale greyish upperparts and dark underparts is distinctive. Despite its name and appearance it is not closely related to true badgers, but is in fact a member of the weasel family. The Honey Badger moves with a lumbering trot, stopping now and again to dig vigorously, with great precision, to unearth prey. It has an anal pouch that produces an asphyxiating stench, the main function of which may be to calm honeybees when raiding nests, as it is seldom used in defence. It also has thick, loose skin that enables the animal to twist and fight back if pinned down by a predator; in this way it is even able to repel Lions. The Honey Badger has a fearless reputation and often preys on snakes, individuals developing a remarkable resistance to snake venom during a lifetime. After a 6-month gestation 1–2 young are born, blind and helpless, in a burrow; they require several months of care before they are able to forage for themselves.

☐ **Black-backed Jackal** *Canis mesomelas*

Size: HB 65–90 cm; Tail 26–40 cm

Weight: 5·9–12 kg (♂ heavier than ♀)

Key identification features: Fox-like, with pointed muzzle and upright ears. Dark saddle grizzled with silver flecking on mostly reddish-brown body. The tail is bushy with a black tip.

Habitat: Grassland and open savannah.

Habits: Mainly nocturnal. Monogamous pairs. Territorial.

Diet: Generalist opportunist. Small mammals, birds, reptiles, invertebrates and carrion.

Smaller than Spotted Hyena and African Wild Dog, this fox-like animal is common and widespread throughout Kruger. It is similar to the Side-striped Jackal but has a dark back and reddish legs, a black-tipped tail and lacks a pale stripe along the flanks. This jackal typically forages alone, searching for smaller prey that is often detected using its acute hearing; it stalks and pounces on prey, like a fox. It also frequently scavenges at kills. Pairs defend their territory with evocative howling, any intruders being aggressively expelled (territories are often lost if one of the pair is killed). Males mate-guard females during the breeding season and there are two birthing peaks: one during the wet season, when rodent and insect numbers are highest, and another in the dry season when carrion is more abundant. The 1–6 pups are born in a burrow (which has multiple entrances) and offspring from previous litters may help to rear the young. Whines and yelps are used for communication among mates and pups. The most frequent predators are Leopards, Spotted Hyenas and eagles.

☐ Side-striped Jackal *Canis adustus*

Size: HB 65–77 cm; Tail 31–41 cm

Weight: 7·3–12 kg

Key identification features: Grey-brown with an indistinct pale stripe running from the shoulder to the rump, and usually a white-tipped tail.

Habitat: Thicker woodland and more closed savannah, where Black-backed Jackal is scarce.

Habits: Generally nocturnal but sometimes active during the day. Monogamous pairs. Territorial. Forages alone or in small family groups.

Diet: Omnivorous and opportunistic, with food varying seasonally: includes small mammals, birds, invertebrates, and carrion, as well as fruits and seeds.

This small, silvery, fox-like animal is widespread but uncommon throughout Kruger – most often seen on night drives. It is similar to the Black-backed Jackal but is paler, has a pale stripe along the flanks and almost always a white-tipped tail. Side-striped Jackals have a varied diet, including fruit, and are less predatory than the more aggressive Black-backed Jackal (which they tend to avoid).

Each home range contains a den, which is often an old Aardvark burrow or a termitarium modified with an additional 'escape' hole. Mating occurs in the dry season, and 4–6 pups are born in the den after a 60-day gestation at the onset of the wet season when there is a peak in food abundance. Both parents feed the pups, either via regurgitation or with small food items brought to the den. Sibling rivalry is intense and pups fight to gain dominance. Side-striped Jackals yap like a dog, and do not emit the distinct high-pitched howling of Black-backed Jackals.

☐ **African Wild Dog** *Lycaon pictus*
(Cape Hunting Dog; Painted Wolf)

Size: HB 84–141 cm; Tail 31–42 cm

Weight: 18–35 kg (♂ heavier than ♀)

Key identification features: Tall, thin-legged dog with large, rounded ears and irregular pattern of variable blotches of brown, white, chocolate and black daubs that appear 'painted' on. Variable vertical forehead stripe and fluffy, mostly white, tail are characteristic.

Habitat: Open savannah and plains.

Habits: Diurnal and crepuscular, rarely nocturnal. Obligate pack animal, with strong social structure.

Diet: Specialize in medium-sized antelopes, including Impala and Greater Kudu. Larger prey if the opportunity arises. Rarely scavenges.

Although rare, the African Wild Dog is regularly encountered in central and southern Kruger – and easily identified by

WILD DOG IN DANGER

Classified as Endangered by the IUCN, the African Wild Dog's range is highly fragmented, having suffered a massive contraction. Kruger's population fluctuates naturally, doing better in dry years when prey is easier to capture. However, a spate of wet years can reduce the numbers to just 120–200 individuals in as few as 17 packs. In addition, canine distemper and rabies can affect the population.

its intricate, multi-coloured body pattern and white-tipped tail. It is highly social, living in large family groups. Home ranges are huge, with packs covering distances of up to 50 km a day when searching for food. Hunting forays are often preceded by much excitement, and the hunt itself is highly coordinated. The dogs rely on endurance and stamina and will follow their prey until it is exhausted, at speeds of around 40 km/h for up to an hour. They are amongst the most successful hunters, with around 80% of chases resulting in a kill, compared to just 30% for Lion. Wild Dogs dispatch their quarry quickly, sometimes by

disembowelment. Their sharp, scissor-like premolars shear through meat efficiently, while their large molars are used for crushing bones, enabling them to eat rapidly – a useful strategy when other predators are likely to steal the kill. Feeding follows an unusual order, with the least dominant (sub-adults) eating first, followed by subordinate adults and then adults. This approach benefits the pack as a whole as it improves the survival rate of the weakest individuals, thereby maintaining the large pack size necessary for successful hunting. After feeding, adults return to the den and regurgitate food for the pack members that were unable to join in the hunt: pups, baby-sitters, and the old and infirm. Packs typically comprise 4–9 adults and 4–12 yearlings. Unusually for social carnivores, males remain faithful to their birth packs while females disperse to join new packs. In most packs males outnumber females, and competition to become the dominant (alpha) pair is intense. However, perhaps as the life of every individual is

key to group survival, overt displays of aggression are rare. Mating is brief, usually only involves the alpha pair, and can occur at any time of year. Gestation lasts 80 days and a litter of up to 19 pups is born in the den. After weaning, the pups are cared for by the entire pack; they begin to run with the pack at three months are not effective hunters until they are a year old.

DOG DAY AFTERNOON
African Wild Dogs rely mostly on sight and need light to hunt. They prefer the cooler hours around dawn and dusk, but will also hunt if there is enough moonlight. They will also move and interact throughout the day, but activity subsides during the hottest part of the day.

PAINTED FINGERPRINTS
The patterns on the fur is unique to each animal, allowing for individual identification.

☐ Temminck's Ground Pangolin *Smutsia temminckii*
(Scaly Anteater; Pangolin)

Size: HB 45–55 cm; Tail 40–52 cm	
Weight: 5–17 kg (♂ heavier than ♀)	
Key identification features: Upper body, broad tail and legs armoured with plated scales. Triangular head; pointed nose; lacks external ears.	
Habitat: Open and scrubby savannah and riverine woodland.	
Habits: Mostly nocturnal. Solitary and terrestrial.	
Diet: Ants and termites, preferring eggs and larvae.	

THE ROLLER
When threatened and sleeping a Pangolin rolls up into a ball, using the hard, overlapping plates on its body to protect its vulnerable underparts. The name is derived from the Malay *peng-goling*, meaning 'the roller'.

PANGOLIN PROBLEMS
Temminck's Ground Pangolin is classified as Vulnerable by the IUCN. It is declining for a number of reasons: being hunted by humans for its 'purported' medicinal value; electrocution through contact with electric fences; and collisions with road traffic.

This scaly anteater is rare in Kruger, and one of the most difficult animals to see due to its secretive nature – resting up in burrows or termitaria during the day and emerging at night. The animal moves slowly when foraging, sniffing in nooks and crannies for its insect prey, sometimes walking on just its hind legs, using its tail as a counterbalance. It feeds almost exclusively on termites and ants, excavating their mounds and nests using powerful forelegs and, in particular, a hardened long third claw on each of the forefeet. The toothless lower jaw is weak and the extremely long tongue, covered with sticky saliva, is flicked out repeatedly to lick up prey. Pangolins are solitary and only associate during mating. Gestation takes five months and a single baby, known as a 'pangopup', is born in the burrow. The 'pup' is weaned at about three months and stays with its mother until sexually mature at two years.

■ Aardvark *Orycteropus afer*

Size: HB 94–142 cm; Tail 44–63 cm

Weight: 40–65 kg

Key identification features: Large, grey-brown animal with dark legs and an arched back. Long, tapering tail, angular head with a long snout and long, hare-like ears. Often soil-stained.

Habitat: Varied; occurs wherever ants and termites are plentiful.

Habits: Poorly known. Nocturnal. Forages alone. Excavates own burrow, in which it spends the day.

Diet: Almost exclusively ants and termites, but sometimes beetle larvae.

This distinctive 'pig-like' anteater is scarce in Kruger, very secretive, and rarely seen, even on night drives. It specializes in feeding on ants and termites, particularly *Anoplolepis* ants and *Trinervitermes* and *Hodotermes* termites. Most of an Aardvark's time above ground is spent foraging, an individual often covering several kilometres each night. Aardvarks trundle along with their nose just above the ground and their ears directed downward, listening for prey, although a huge olfactory lobe in the brain suggests that a sense of smell is also important in prey location. They dig with their front feet, which have flattened claws that resemble shovels. Aardvarks have a long tongue, which can be extended 30 cm to collect prey, that is kept sticky by a ring of salivary glands around the mouth. The teeth and digestive systems are highly modified for rapid food processing.

Otters

Otters dispatch smaller prey underwater, whereas larger items are dismembered and eaten at the surface. They excavate their own resting places, called holts, under rocks, among roots, or similar sites close to water, which are also used by females for giving birth. Mating can occur any time, but births peak in the wet season. Gestation lasts 60 days and the pups (usually 1–3), which are blind at birth, suckle for 60 days before joining their mother on hunting forays, leaving to go their own way after about a year. The males play no role in parental care.

☐ Spotted-necked Otter *Hydrictis maculicollis*

Size: HB 57–76 cm; Tail 38–44 cm

Weight: ♂ 5·7–6·0 kg, ♀ 3.8–4.7 kg

Key identification features: Slightly smaller with proportionately longer and slimmer body than African Clawless Otter. Dark head, including cheeks, and variable dark and pale mottling on the throat.

Habitat: Freshwater rivers, dams and swamps with adjacent vegetation. Prefers shallow water.

Habits: Diurnal and crepuscular, avoiding the more nocturnal African Clawless Otter. Solitary or small family groups forage together.

Diet: Fishes, frogs, crustaceans, sometimes birds and insects.

This medium-sized otter is very rare in Kruger, and seldom seen. It is similar to the African Clawless Otter but is smaller and has much darker cheeks and a mottled throat. The Spotted-necked Otter hunts by sight, foraging close to the shore with short dives of around 20 seconds. Prey is generally caught with the mouth, hard-bodied prey sometimes being smashed open against a rock. In winter, fish smaller than 20 cm are preferred as they move more slowly in cold water; in the wet season frogs and crabs are more frequent prey. Although typically a solitary animal, feeding success may increase when individuals forage cooperatively.

African Clawless Otter *Aonyx capensis*
(Cape Clawless Otter)

Size: HB 73–88 cm; Tail 47–52 cm

Weight: ♂ 10–21 kg, ♀ 10–16 kg

Key identification features: Large, dark-backed otter with diagnostic white cheeks extending from under the ear and onto the throat and upper breast. A dark muzzle smudge extends off the bridge of the nose under the eyes.

Habitat: Riverine areas with dense adjacent cover, often near boulders or reedbeds. May traverse drier terrain.

Habits: Nocturnal and crepuscular, but sometimes active during the day. Usually solitary, but can occur in small clans. Semi-territorial, but ranges may overlap and clans may defend joint territories.

Diet: Primarily crabs, but also frogs and fishes, as well as other invertebrates.

Scarce and seldom seen in Kruger, this large otter is similar to the Spotted-necked Otter but has much whiter cheeks. It is a water-loving species with webbed hindfeet and, as its name suggests, lacks claws (although it does have small grooming claws on the hindfeet). In murky water they are tactile foragers, using their feet to feel for prey in crevices and cavities, but in clearer water look for prey and plunge-dive to catch it with their forefeet. It is a highly mobile predator, foraging over many kilometres each day.

OTTER ISSUES
Africa's wetlands are threatened by pollution, invasive species, and climate change. Although this has an impact on otters, they also suffer from disturbance due to increased human pressure. This has led to a decline in both otter species in the last 20 years, and as a result the status of both has recently been changed to Near Threatened by the IUCN.

☐ **African Elephant** *Loxodonta africana*

Size: HB 600–750 cm; Tail 100–150 cm

Weight: ♂ 3–6 tonnes, ♀ 1–3 tonnes

Key identification features: Giant, hairless, grey mammal with huge ears, long prehensile trunk, and large, ivory tusks.

Habitat: Most habitats, but highest densities in woodlands.

Habits: Active during day and night, with naps taken throughout the 24-hour cycle, though more often after dark. Feeding is the main activity, with up to 450 kg of vegetation being consumed over 17 hours/day. Highly social, with complex relationships.

Diet: Generalist browser on a wide variety of grasses and trees, including roots, bark, leaves, stalks, stems, fruits and seeds, depending on availability.

Elephants are huge and unmistakable, and a frequent sight throughout Kruger. Having evolved from pig-like swamp-dwellers some 50 million years ago, Earth's largest terrestrial mammal is justly famous. With its highly developed brain, it ranks alongside primates and dolphins as one of the most intelligent animals. Elephants exhibit a wide variety of behaviours associated with complex intelligence, including grief, learning, adopting babies if their own mothers cannot care for them, tool use, compassion, cooperation, self-awareness, strong memory, and possibly even language.

The elephant's large ears are essential for thermoregulation. When the animal is hot, blood is pushed through the flapping ears to increase cooling. The modified upper lip and nose form a sensitive tactile trunk capable of grasping and manipulating

items with incredible precision. Whenever possible Elephants feed on grass, but switch to leaves in the dry season when grass is less nutritious; their specially adapted digestive system allowing them to metabolize low-quality forage. African Elephants have four enormous molars, each tooth weighing close to 5 kg, which are shed when they wear out. These are replaced 4–6 times during an animal's lifetime. Many elephants die after suffering from malnutrition and succumbing to disease because they no longer have functional teeth. The second set of incisors is modified to form tusks, which are used for fighting, especially among males, and also as tools with which to prise bark off trees or dig for tubers and roots.

Males are told from females by larger tusks and a bulbous, rounded forehead; in females (*opposite*), the forehead is strongly angular.

Tusks continue to grow throughout an elephant's life and so-called 'Big Tuskers' are usually animals over 40 years old.

Elephant relationships are complex and managed by closely related females (termed matriarchal societies). In such societies, the leader, or matriarch, is usually an older female and there are multiple hierarchical levels beneath her; the degree of relatedness to the matriarch normally dictating status. However, the nature of elephant hierarchy remains poorly understood, and is the subject of ongoing scientific research. After puberty, males form strong alliances with other males, and move away to live separately from the females and calves. During seasonal

One of the BIG 5

peaks of females entering breeding condition, older, dominant males enter a heightened physiological sexual state known as 'musth'. In this state, a male will often leave the bachelor herd and wander alone, becoming more aggressive, releasing pungent pheromones, dribbling urine, and having swollen temporal glands. Females in breeding condition will offer males in 'musth' temporary access for mating, but otherwise will excluded them from the herd. Oestrus lasts 2–3 days and, following successful mating, pregnancy lasts 22 months – the longest gestation of any mammal. Calves are highly dependent upon their mothers, which provide constant maternal care and as a consequence are unlikely to fall pregnant again for 3–4 years. Young elephants learn much about how to survive from the adults in their herd.

THE STATUS OF KRUGER'S ELEPHANTS

The African Elephant is considered globally threatened, and classified as Vulnerable by the IUCN. This is largely because of the illegal trade in ivory and poaching throughout Africa. In 1994, the culling of elephants was banned in South Africa, and since then the population in Kruger has doubled, reaching 16,000 individuals by 2014. Culling was reintroduced as a policy in 2008, but it has not been practiced. However, since Kruger's carrying capacity is thought to be closer to 8,000 individuals, and because fences around the park prevent elephants from migrating, it is possible the park's more sensitive habitats are being damaged as a result of excessive grazing pressure. The proposed creation of larger conservation areas capable of sustaining more elephants is good news, but some proponents of culling argue that the elephants will have a detrimental effect on local biodiversity if control measures are not implemented soon. Either way, this is a controversial subject that has stirred the emotions of the public.

Females are among Kruger's most devoted parents and babies seldom stray more than a few meters from their protective mother (*above*). Elephants frequently engage in mud-bathing to protect their skin from the sun and parasites (*below*).

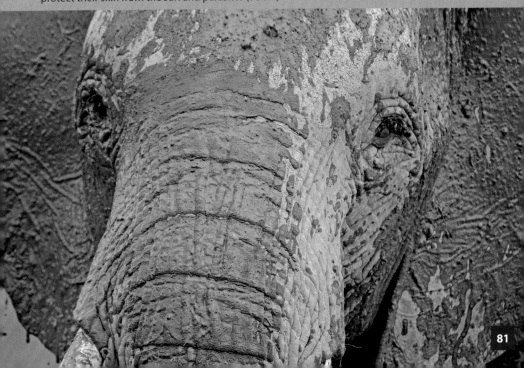

RHINOS

Rhinos first appeared in Asia during the Eocene, about 50 million years ago (MYA), where three species still persist. Rhinos were present in Africa by about 10 MYA, and the two African species separated from a common ancestor around 5 MYA. The characteristic horns, which grow throughout their lives, are used for defence and intimidation, and for digging up roots and breaking branches when feeding. Thick plate-like skin protects rhinos from thorns and parasites, and the animals also often wallow in mud to protect themselves from parasites, and to cool down.

☐ White Rhinoceros *Ceratotherium simum*
(Square-lipped Rhinoceros)

Size: HB 340–420 cm; Tail 50–70 cm

Weight: 1·3–3·5 tonnes
(♂ heavier than ♀)

Key identification features: Huge, hairless, bulky, greyish, with two horns; larger than Black Rhino (*page 84*). Told from Black Rhino by broad, square lips; more elongated, narrow head; and strongly notched ears. Bulges on the back are more pronounced than in the Black Rhino. Calves run in front of the mother.

Habitat: Lighter savannah and open grassland, preferring short grass.

Habits: Diurnal and nocturnal. The most social rhino; females and young will coalesce in groups. Males are solitary. Territorial: male territory 9·9 km², female 22·8 km². Drinks regularly.

Diet: Grazes grass.

The White Rhino is fairly common in the south and central parts of Kruger, with the population estimated at 6,000–8,000 individuals. It is similar to Black Rhino but larger and has distinctive square lips. Males are much bigger than females, although females tend to have longer and thinner horns. Males compete for core territories that provide the best grazing and water, marking them by spraying urine and depositing faeces regularly at large dung piles (middens). They will try to retain and mate with any female that visits their territory to forage. Copulation is protracted, taking up to 30 minutes, and the pair associates closely for 5–20 days before splitting up. The single calf is born after a 17-month gestation. After 2–3 years, the female becomes receptive again and will expel the previous calf shortly before or soon after the next birth.

The extremely wide mouth of the White Rhino is the best way to tell it from the Black Rhino.

One of the BIG 5

Black Rhinoceros *Diceros bicornis*
(Hooked-lipped Rhinoceros)

Size: HB 300–380 cm; Tail 25–35 cm

Weight: 0·8–1·3 tonnes

Key identification features: Huge, bulky, hairless, greyish, with two horns; smaller than White Rhino (*page 82*). The prehensile upper lip is 'V'-shaped when viewed from the front. More compact head often held aloft, ears rounded and 'trumpet-like', and hollow saddle on the back. Calf runs behind the mother.

Habitat: Thickets and thorny dry-savannah; avoids open grassland.

Habits: Mostly solitary, only forming pairs to breed. Strong bond between mother and calf. Forages and drinks in early morning and evenings.

Diet: Browses on a variety of plants, including thorn trees, and also eats fruits.

Uncommon and secretive, the Black Rhino is mostly restricted to the south and central parts of Kruger, with a population numbering around 600 individuals. It is smaller than White Rhino and has a hooked (rather than square), dexterous upper lip, which is used to grasp vegetation and branches when foraging. They have very poor eyesight and rely on smell and hearing when going about their daily routines. Black Rhinos are not particularly territorial but are highly strung and will readily fight to the death. Mating can occur year-round and is a quite violent process. Gestation takes 16 months and females give birth to a calf every 3–4 years; at times two calves can be seen accompanying the mother. Crocodiles, Spotted Hyenas and Lions may predate calves, but these predators risk a serious mauling from the extremely protective mothers.

RHINOS – THREATS AND NAMES

POACHING

Rhinos are in serious trouble, and not for the first time. White Rhinos were brought back from the brink of extinction in 1894, when only 50 animals remained in KwaZulu-Natal, South Africa. By 2010 they numbered around 20,000, 18,000 of which were in South Africa. Unfortunately, a new poaching era has begun, and in 2013 and 2014 this claimed the lives of 1,004 and 1,020 rhinos respectively. Of those, more than 600 animals were killed in Kruger each year – equivalent to one rhino every 11 hours. The rise of upper- and middle-class consumers in Vietnam and the Far East has increased demand for powdered horn, which is taken as a remedy for hangovers and because it purportedly has medicinal properties, all of which have been refuted repeatedly by medical science. Despite over 300 arrests, army and drone deployment, and helicopter patrols, the slaughter continues. It is unsustainable, and this is a worrying time for African rhinos. It seems that the only real solution lies in educating the people driving the demand.

Black Rhinos have a pointed upper lip (square on White Rhino).

If you want to help rhinos, please consider making a donation to Breaking the Brand (http://breakingthebrand.org/), an NGO that is changing perceptions about rhino horn in Vietnam, the most important market. The Black Rhino is classified as Critically Endangered and the White Rhino as Near Threatened – although this will almost certainly be changed to at least Vulnerable when the next IUCN assessment is completed.

WHAT'S IN A NAME?

A bit of a misnomer, the White Rhino's name is thought to come from English-speakers misinterpreting the Dutch word, meaning wide, which was supposedly used to describe the animal's broad lips. It is assumed that the Black Rhino gained its name by default. The names Square-lipped (instead of White), and Hooked-lipped (instead of Black) are better descriptors and perhaps should be more widely used.

☐ **Hippopotamus** *Hippopotamus amphibious*

Size: HB 290–505 cm; Tail 40–56 cm

Weight: ♂ 1·5–1·8 tonnes,
♀ 1·3–1·5 tonnes

Key identification features: Large, podgy, cylindrical body, with short limbs and large head. Small eyes and ears on the top of a broad, heavy-jawed mouth and snout. Skin is pinkish-grey.

Habitat: Freshwater rivers and dams surrounded by suitable grazing.

Habits: Aquatic by day in gregarious herds (or pods) numbering 15–300. Each herd of 10–15 has a dominant male, with several females and calves. Bachelor herds also occur. Basks on riverbanks when the sun is not too intense. Solitary or small groups are terrestrial grazers at night, wandering away from water.

Diet: Primarily grazers of short, green grass near their wetland homes, eating up to 30–40 kg/night. Has been observed eating aquatic vegetation and flesh at carcasses.

This large and portly animal is common throughout Kruger, with a population of some 3,000 individuals. It is regularly found in permanent water (*e.g.* large rivers and dams) and sometimes seen on riverbanks by day, or grazing in adjacent grassy savannah after dark. At a distance, a Hippo could conceivably be confused with a rhino, but lacks horns.

Hippos are remarkably well adapted to an aquatic lifestyle, having muscular valves that automatically seal the nose the instant it touches water, and ears, eyes and nostrils on the top of the head – allowing them to hear, see and breathe while being 98% submerged. Hippos mostly walk on the bottom of lakes and riverbeds, as they neither float nor swim very well. The pillar-like limbs are adapted to support the immense bodyweight of the animal out of the water, which is where Hippos do most of their foraging. They use their muscular lips to pluck grass, and have an efficient foregut fermentation process that extracts most of the nutrients from what they eat.

To acquire the bacteria that drive this fermentation, young hippos must first eat the faeces of other Hippos. The greasy skin is thick but sensitive to the sun. Hippos perspire an acidic, reddish compound called 'blood sweat' that acts as both an antibiotic against infections from skin abrasions, and a sunscreen that absorbs damaging ultraviolet light.

Hippos can appear extremely fearsome and intimidating, especially when opening their mouths to a maximum gape of 180° and revealing massive, 40–50 cm-long, front teeth. This is a common threat display and as the animal performs it, the teeth grind against each other forming sharpened sabres. These are deadly weapons which are used during fights. To gain control over females, males will challenge one another to 'gaping contests', which can boil over into severe clashes and result in serious injury. Each female gives birth to a single calf about every two years, after an eight-month gestation, and the youngster suckles for almost a year before becoming independent.

THREATS AND DANGERS

A Hippo's portly demeanour is deceptive, since it is able to run at 30km/h and can easily outstrip a human. Rightly regarded as Africa's most dangerous large mammal, Hippos can be locally common near protected areas, where they often come into contact with, and attack, people who use the rivers for transport and food. This inevitably results in conflict and often results in Hippos being killed. Hippos are particularly prone to drought, as their sensitive skin cannot withstand desiccation – and when wetlands dry out they can die in droves. Their cantankerous nature means that Hippo's generally escape the attentions of predators, although they are occasionally killed by Lions. As a result of the many threats facing African wetlands, and persecution by man, the Hippo is considered to be globally threatened and classified as Vulnerable by the IUCN.

HIPPO HISTORY

The closest living relatives of the Hippo are whales and dolphins. Their ancestors diverged from one another around 55 million years ago (MYA), and around 16 MYA the hippo lineage began to resemble modern Hippos. As recently as the last ice age there were several other hippo species in existence, three of which were on Madagascar, where they were driven to extinction. Today, there are only two extant species (the Hippo and the Pygmy Hippo *Choeropsis liberiensis*), both of which are restricted to Africa.

HIPPO = HAPPY FISH

Hippos play a key role in maintaining open water channels and ensuring high aquatic diversity. Their faeces alter the chemical composition of the water, which appears to be essential in maintaining fish diversity and productive fisheries. Hippos also visit 'cleaning stations' where certain fish species remove parasites from the insides of their mouths, to the benefit of both parties.

The Hippo is perfectly adapted to life in water, being able to keep its body submerged and protected from the harsh sun while its ears, eyes and nose all remain above water.

Common Warthog *Phacochoerus africanus*

Size: HB 105–150 cm; Tail 35–50 cm

Weight: ♂ 60–150 kg, ♀ 50–75 kg

Key identification features: Long-legged, short-necked, grey-brown pig; mostly hairless but with a hairy mane extending from head to spine. Muzzle flat, replete with warts and a pair of large, curved, upward-pointing tusks. Tusks larger in male, reaching 30 cm. Long tail with a tufted end, held erect like a car aerial when alarmed or running.

Habitat: Open grassland and woodland savannah near permanent water.

Habits: Diurnal, retiring to shelter to spend the night. Males accompany females during breeding, but otherwise bachelor groups, or groups of females with piglets (sounders), are typical. Not territorial, but has a home range.

Diet: Omnivorous: primarily roots, tubers, and rhizomes in the dry season; grass, fruits, bark, and fungi in the wet season; and opportunistically eggs, carrion, reptiles, birds and small mammals.

This small pig is common in Kruger, with numbers estimated at around 4,000 individuals. It is diurnal, grey in colour and runs with tail raised; males have prominent warts on their snout and long tusks. It could be confused with the **Bushpig** *Potamochoerus larvatus* (rare in Kruger; not illustrated), which is nocturnal, reddish-brown with a mane of light hair, has small tusks and runs with its tail down. When rooting and foraging Warthogs often drop onto their knees, which have callosities for protection. They use their hard snouts, rather than their tusks, to dig up roots, rhizomes and tubers, eating whatever happens to be plentiful. Warthogs manage their body temperatures by wallowing, dust-bathing and sheltering in the shade. To escape from high temperatures and to hide their young they make use of deep burrows, such as an old Aardvark burrow.

ALTERNATIVE IVORY

Warthog tusks are used as an alternative to ivory and carved for the tourist trade. At present, such use is sustainable and is beneficial in supporting local artisans.

Males will 'reverse' into the burrow when going to sleep so that any potential threat is faced by a pair of lethal tusks. Warthogs are seasonal breeders, with rutting taking place in the dry season and births peaking during the rains. Both sexes are promiscuous and although males generally try to mate with as many females as possible, some will try to mate-guard; fights often ensue between males attempting to get first access to females in breeding condition. Gestation lasts about six months, and 2–5 young are born in a burrow. Piglets venture out after 2–3 weeks and are weaned by six months. Females are fearless mothers and will fight to protect their offspring – there are even records of Lions being gored and killed as a result. Nonetheless, Warthogs feature regularly on the menus of many of Kruger's apex predators.

One of the Warthog's adaptations to a grass and root diet is very long hind molars. As a result the face is longer than that of other pigs.

HOG HYGIENE

Warthogs have been observed allowing Banded Mongooses and ground-hornbills to glean ticks off them, although such behaviour is far from commonplace.

Plains Zebra *Equus quagga*

Size: HB 217–246 cm; Tail 47–57 cm

Weight: 175–320 kg

Key identification features: Distinctive black-and-white striped horse. Often with shadow-stripes.

Habitat: Open and closed savannah with good grazing and water nearby.

Habits: Diurnal and nocturnal, activities centred around daily drinking. Stallion has a harem with foals. Not territorial, responding to temporary food sources. Male will mate-guard.

Diet: Grazers preferring grasses, especially Red Grass, but will also browse Mopane and other trees and shrubs. Favours fresh growth in post-burn areas.

This unmistakable black-and-white horse is common in Kruger, with a population estimated at more than 26,000. Zebras digest their plant food by a hindgut fermentation process, which means they must feed for up to 20 hours a day to consume a large enough quantity to survive. Their need to drink daily means they seldom wander farther than 10 km from permanent water during the dry winter months. During the wet season they disperse, exploiting temporary water and grazing. Zebras have a complex social structure, regularly issuing the characteristic "*a-ha-ha, a-ha-ha, a-ha-ha*" contact call. Herds either comprise bachelor groups or dominant males with harems with group size being influenced

by local grazing conditions. Bachelors will not turn down the opportunity of mating with females in a dominant stallion's harem if they get the chance. Females associating with a dominant (alpha) male benefit from less harassment and thus have more time for foraging. A single foal is born after a one-year gestation and remains with its mother and stays close to the herd; it suckles for six months but starts grazing after a month.

HOW DID THE ZEBRA GET ITS STRIPES?

No two Zebras look alike and individuals can be identified using their patterns. Many theories have attempted to explain the purpose of the stripes. One theory is camouflage in woodlands, but given the species' bold nature and preference for open habitats this seems unlikely. Another is that the visual interference created by the black-and-white stripes of a herd in motion may confuse those predators (such as Lion) with reduced colour vision. However, scientific research has rejected both assertions and it seems that the pattern either acts as a social cue, or polarizes light, which repels flies such as the dangerous Tsetse flies that transmit the ungulate disease Nagana (similar to sleeping sickness in humans).

Plains Zebras do not wander too far from water as they prefer to drink daily.

Giraffe *Giraffa camelopardalis*

Size: HB 350–480 cm; Tail 76–110 cm

Weight: ♂ 1·8 tonnes, ♀ 0·5–1·1 tonnes

Key identification features: Long-legged, long-necked, camel-like animal with small head. Two tufted stumps on the top of the head; males' stumps are bald on top, females' are covered in fine hair.

Habitat: Savannah and open woodland, with tall, scattered trees for browsing.

Habits: Diurnal. Not territorial. Mothers and calves have strong bonds, but other relationships are flexible and members will join or depart without commitment. Polygamous.

Diet: Grazes on leaves and sprouting branches of thorn trees like *Vachellia* (formerly *Acacia*), *Commiphora* and *Terminalia*; eats around 34 kg of vegetation per day.

This unmistakable large and bizarre animal is fairly common in Kruger, with a population estimated at around 7,500. It is the world's tallest terrestrial mammal, standing 5–6 m, and the largest ruminant. Like almost all mammals, the Giraffe only has seven neck vertebrae – but these are disproportionately large, each measuring some 28 cm in length, resulting in the longest and stiffest neck in the world. Several other physiological adaptations are required to keep a Giraffe's head in the sky: the blood pressure is twice that of similar-sized animals, the cells in the walls of the heart are larger, and the heart rate is around 150 beats per minute. It also has an organ at the base of the skull that regulates blood flow so that there is neither too much nor too little blood reaching the brain when it lifts or lowers its head.

GIRAFFE FAMILY TREE

The bizarre Okapi *Okapia johnstoni* of the Congo Basin is the only other member in the Giraffe family, and their next closest relative is the Pronghorn *Antilocapra americana* of North America. There used to be many Giraffe relatives around the globe, but around seven million years ago, as the African savannahs expanded and giraffes moved in, the Eurasian and North American species died out.

Due to their extended necks, Giraffes can easily reach food that is not available to other large savannah mammals. The dexterous 50 cm-long tongue, which has the texture of sandpaper, allows the animal to tear reams of small compound leaves off thorn trees without damaging their mouth. In order to ruminate, extraordinarily powerful oesophageal muscles are used to return the cud to the mouth. Giraffes require less food for their size than other ruminants because of their high-nutrient diet and efficient digestive system.

The brown and white patches across a Giraffe's body are distinctive and unique to each individual. These were once thought to be a camouflage mechanism, but Giraffes are hard to miss! Beneath the 'browner' patches, the skin contains complex networks of blood vessels and large sweat glands, suggesting that these patches are used for thermoregulation (controlling heat loss/gain).

Giraffes are mostly solitary, but males and females associate for breeding. Males will indulge in 'necking' contests, swinging and slamming their long necks against one another with considerable force, often

injuring the fighters. The victors of these battles are the dominant animals and get to mate with the most females. Gestation takes 13–15 months, and the single calf (rarely twins), which already measures 1·8 m at birth, remains with its mother until the next calf is born.

Adult Giraffes are not normally subject to predation, but are sometimes killed by Lions – although the involvement of large male Lions in the hunt is typically required. It is a dangerous business, though, as a blow to the Lion's head or jaw by a Giraffe's powerful hind legs could easily end the big cat's life. Giraffes are ungainly, but can run at 50 km/h for several kilometres. In order to catch a Giraffe, Lions must either corner it in habitat through which it cannot gallop, or ambush it. Giraffes are most vulnerable to attack when they drink, as they need to splay their front legs awkwardly in order reach the water. Consequently, they take a long time to survey the scene before committing to drink. Other predators, such as Leopard, Spotted Hyena and African Wild Dog tend to prey on calves.

WHY ARE GIRAFFES SO WEIRD?
Scientists have come up with a range of intriguing explanations for the strangeness of the Giraffe. Some have hypothesized that as Africa's savannahs opened up, new plants, including thorn trees with physical and chemical defences, exposed these animals to a spike in toxins, which then increased mutation rates and brought about the evolutionary development of this weird and wonderful enigma. This does sound rather like science fiction, though! Others suggest that their long necks evolved as a result of sexual selection, with longer-necked males winning more neck-bashing contests.

A male Giraffe (*above*) has bald stumps on its head, whereas females (*opposite*) have tufts. The thick, leathery tongue (*below*) enables a Giraffe to strip nutritional leaves off thorny branches.

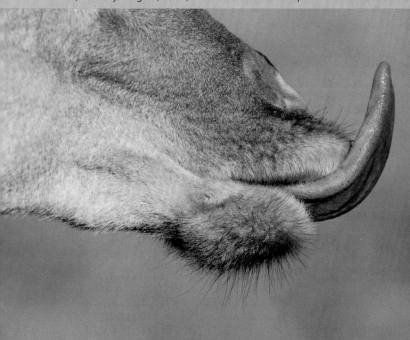

☐ African Buffalo *Syncerus caffer*

Size: HB 240–340 cm; Tail 50–110 cm

Weight: ♂ 500–900 kg, ♀ 350–620 kg

Key identification features: Huge, blackish-brown, ox-like animal with a pair of large, laterally splayed horns that arc downwards and then recurve.

Habitat: Open and closed woodland, with access to grazing and permanent water.

Habits: Diurnal and nocturnal, with 75% of a 24-hour day spent feeding and resting. Complex social structure; herds comprise female clans accompanied by males, and groups of bachelor males.

Diet: Prefers grass, eating about 14 kg/day. Browses more during the dry season.

BUFFALO FAMILY TREE

Although superficially similar to other bovines, the African Buffalo is only distantly related to them and their evolutionary history is uncertain. Bovines arose 20 million years ago, and although the two main groups evolved in isolation in Eurasia and Africa, they mixed and dispersed when the continents were later reconnected. The African Buffalo's closest relatives are all Eurasian, which suggests that its ancestors colonized Africa from Eurasia, rather than originating and evolving in Africa.

The massive African Buffalo is the second most common ungulate in Kruger after the Impala. It is also the most frequently encountered of the 'Big 5', with some 40,000 individuals inhabiting the park. The African Buffalo's front legs and hooves

One of the BIG 5

The African Buffalo's position in the 'Big 5' is well earned, as it is arguably the most dangerous mammal in Africa. They have an unpredictable temperament and there are many records of people being attacked – especially game hunters, which they have been known to ambush. Buffalos favour thick bush, and by the time people realize there are buffalos nearby, it is too late.

are larger than those at the back in order to support the heavier forequarters. The bases of the massive horns are fused into a bony shield called a 'boss' that is thick enough to stop a bullet! The tips of the horns can be one metre apart in large males. As this species has to drink daily, it needs to remain close to permanent water. It is a capable swimmer, sometimes crossing deep water to locate better grazing. Its grass diet provides the bulk of its nutritional requirements but lacks some important trace elements. These need to be obtained separately, either at salt licks around pans, or by licking salt off the hides of other buffalos that has been deposited when wallowing.

Buffalo society is complex: herd size varies from five to over 100, but the core social unit consists of related females and their offspring. Females and their daughters dominate, while subordinate males and old or injured animals remain on the periphery. Males may form bachelor herds in the dry season, but they rejoin the core herds when the females come into breeding condition. At this time the bulls spar for dominance and, although much of the action is ritualized, there are occasional serious clashes with horns being used to gore competitors. Buffalo hide can be up to 6 cm thick in places, which helps to protect the internal organs during such contests. Once male dominance is established mating commences, although cows are quite evasive and commonly copulate with more than one male. It seems that births in Kruger tend to peak 12–13 months after an increase in good grazing, suggesting that breeding is determined by female condition at conception. New calves are hidden in the bush for a few weeks, joining the herd, from which they receive protection, when they are strong enough.

Once independent, young males leave their group and join bachelor herds or herds led by unrelated females; in contrast, young females are incorporated into their maternal herd. Buffalos are unusual in that they engage in communal decision-making that is independent of hierarchy and status, especially regarding the choice of foraging areas. The study of the mechanism by which they arrive at their decisions is still in its infancy and is not well understood.

BUFFALO BODYGUARDS

Buffalos are highly protective of other herd members. Unlike most other ungulates, they will return to rescue animals that are being attacked by predators. A famous and incredible example is the 'Battle at Kruger' video on YouTube, widely regarded as some of the most remarkable amateur wildlife footage ever caught on camera. In this video a young African Buffalo is attacked by Lions and Nile Crocodiles – but these predators did not bargain for the reaction they got from the little buffalo's family!

Wallowing in mud (*above*) helps African Buffalos protect their hide and shed unwanted parasites. A darker, larger-horned male stands next to a smaller, browner female (*below*).

Common Eland *Tragelaphus oryx*

Size: HB ♂ 250–340 cm, ♀ 200–280 cm; Tail 54–75 cm

Weight: ♂ 400–942 kg, ♀ 390–600 kg

Key identification features: Massive shoulders and deep chest. Smallish head with short, tightly spiralled horns and a loose dewlap on the throat. Uniform beige fur. Characteristic dark patches on the back of the forelegs.

Habitat: Open savannah and woodland. Avoids swamps and thicker habitat.

Habits: Nomadic, moving to where forage is best. Highly variable herd size, lacking long-term stability. Forage and ruminate in spells throughout day, and at night if temperatures are warm enough. Not tied to standing water, extracting most water from their food.

Diet: A browser, eating leaves and fruits, but will graze early in the wet season when grasses are most palatable.

This large, pale antelope is uncommon in Kruger, with a population estimated at around 450 individuals. It is the world's second largest antelope after the Giant Eland *Tragelaphus derbianus* of West Africa. The name eland is derived from the old Dutch word for Elk or Moose, the name given to it by Africa's colonial settlers. Despite its bulk, it is a sleek and elegant animal, and although one of the slowest antelopes, being built more for cruising than for speed, can jump an impressive 2·5 m from a standing start.

The Common Eland's social structure is unusual, presumably because it is nomadic. Although individuals gather when feeding, there are no real bonds and these are associations of convenience. Juveniles and females form larger herds, while males join small bachelor groups or roam as loners. The sexes associate briefly when females come into breeding condition, with females typically selecting the largest and most dominant bull. Male hierarchies are established by fighting, but these disputes tend to be settled without much violence. A single calf is born after a gestation of nine months and soon joins the other calves within the herd as part of a nursery group, relying for protection against predators on communal defence by the females. The Common Eland's large size means that only the largest and most social predators (Lions, African Wild Dogs and Spotted Hyenas) attempt to hunt them, normally focussing only on the young.

The male (*above*) is told from the female (*below*) by its larger dewlap, thicker horns and more hair on the forehead.

ELAND MILK ANYONE?

The leather, meat and milk of the Common Eland are used by numerous tribes. Eland has also been domesticated in many areas, including South Africa and Russia.

☐ **Greater Kudu** *Tragelaphus strepsiceros*

Size: HB ♂ 213–248 cm, ♀ 205–217 cm; Tail 41–75 cm

Weight: ♂ 190–270 kg, ♀ 120–210 kg

Key identification features: Large, tall antelope with long legs. Brown fur with vertical whitish stripes. Large, rounded ears give the head a 'Y'-shaped profile when seen from the front. Pale white chevron on nose. Only male has long (normally over 1 m), wide, spiralling horns, and a 'throat fringe'.

Habitat: Riverine forest, woodland and thicket, preferring thornveld and bushwillows.

Habits: Territorial, with overlapping home ranges. Active both day and night, foraging for up to 85% of the time, although there are marked seasonal shifts; when temperatures are high forages more at night. Not tied to water, extracting most of the water needed from its food.

Diet: Browser, eating leaves, flowers, and fruits of over 60 plant species; choice varies seasonally. Rarely eats grass.

The Greater Kudu is a large, tall, stately antelope that is common in Kruger, with a population estimated at more than 15,000. In order to sustain themselves, they need to process almost 40 kg of food a day, a task made easier as they can browse a wide range of vegetation not available to most other antelopes. Kudus can reach vegetation up to 1·7 m above ground, can tolerate plant toxins and cope with other plant defences such as thorns.

In Kruger, male Kudus favour riverine areas all year round; females frequent hilly areas in the wet season and riverine areas during the dry season. Males and females form small single-sex groups when not breeding.

Mature males (6–7 years old) dominate subordinate males with displays and ritual horn locking, though violent encounters are unusual. On rare occasions, horns become entangled, resulting in the deaths of both unfortunate animals. Mature males associate with female groups in their home range, though do not have harems. Females may mate with more than one male, although the advances of younger males are typically rebuffed. Male courtship gestures include neck-wrestling, lip-curling (the so-called 'flehmen response'), and resting the head on the female's rump. The timing of breeding in Kruger is highly synchronous, with 85% of the calves being born in January–February after a nine-month gestation. Each female has a single calf, which joins the herd after hiding for 4–5 weeks. Kudus, especially youngsters, are predated by Lions, Leopards, Spotted Hyenas and African Wild Dogs.

Unlike females (*opposite*), male Kudus have distinctive spiralling horns and long hair on the throat.

☐ Common Duiker *Sylvicapra grimmia*
(Bush Duiker; Grey Duiker)

Size: HB ♂ 70–105 cm, ♀ 90–115 cm;
Tail 10–20 cm

Weight: ♂ 9·7–22·4 kg, ♀ 10·3–26·3 kg

Key identification features: Sandy-brown, small to medium-sized antelope with distinctive glandular slits beneath the eyes and dark vertical stripe from forehead to nose. Unique tuft of long, dark hair between the ears. Dark central upper tail, and dark shin stripes on the forelegs. Male has short, straight, sharp black horns approx. 10 cm in length.

Habitat: Prefers riverine areas, rocky outcrops and thicket.

Habits: Diurnal and crepuscular. Mostly solitary, only associating for breeding. Swims. When running, prefers to dart under obstacles rather than jump.

Diet: Browser, preferring leaves, buds and flowers of low-level herbaceous plants and shrubs.

Female Common Duiker is easily identified by the tuft of hair between its ears. Male (*inset*) has small, straight, black horns.

This small brownish antelope is numerous and regularly seen in Kruger. It is told from other small antelope by its greyer coat, dark patch above the nose and distinctive tuft between the ears. Males are territorial and occupy non-overlapping territories, marking boundaries with secretions from a gland near the eye. Several female territories will fall within those of a male. Pairs form during the 2–3-day oestrus, with chasing and biting common prior to mating. A single calf is born after a 200-day gestation, hiding until it is strong enough to join the mother. In their thicket habitat, Common Duikers fall prey to Leopards, Servals, African Wild Dogs, Martial Eagles, Chacma Baboons or Southern African Pythons. They often associate with primates, foraging on dropped fruits.

☐ Sharpe's Grysbok *Raphicerus sharpei*

Size: HB 71–80 cm; Tail 4–7 cm

Weight: 6·4–8·9 kg

Key identification features: Small, reddish-brown antelope with many whitish hairs giving it a diagnostic grizzled appearance. Longer-haired coat imparts a scruffier appearance than similar Steenbok (*page 108*) and it has a broader nasal area. Only male has short, straight, black horns approx. 6 cm in length. When disturbed, has a characteristic habit of slinking away crouched, rather than bounding.

Habitat: Prefers thick bush, often hiding in deep cover, including rocky outcrops and riverine vegetation. More common in northern Kruger than in the south.

Habits: Solitary. Mostly nocturnal, and secretive.

Diet: A wide range of plants; prefers to browse rather than graze.

This secretive antelope is uncommon and seldom seen in Kruger as it prefers impenetrable thicket habitat and is mostly active at night. It is told from Common Duiker by its reddish coloration, and from Steenbok by its more grizzled appearance. Grysboks are most frequently encountered on cooler days, during night drives, or in the early morning when they return to their resting place, such as an Aardvark burrow. Little is known about the biology of this antelope, but males appear to be territorial and utilize dung middens. They have scent glands in the feet, below each eye and in the genital area, suggesting that scent and smell are important for communication. Being nocturnal, their main predators are Leopards. Some consider the east and southern African races to be separate species, and call the animals in Kruger the Limpopo Grysbok *Raphicerus colonicus*.

☐ Steenbok *Raphicerus campestris*

Size: HB 74–75 cm; Tail 5–5·5 cm

Weight: 9–13·2 kg

Key identification features: Small, brown antelope. Similar to Sharpe's Grysbok (*page 107*). Belly white, giving a distinctive two-tone appearance; fur short and sleek. Narrower snout than Sharpe's Grysbok with darker bridge to the nose. Ears patterned on inside. Only male has short, straight, black horns, approx. 9–19 cm in length.

Habitat: Bushed grassland and light woodland, preferring *Vachellia tortilis* thickets and more open habitat than Sharpe's Grysbok.

Habits: Active day and night in monogamous pairs. Territorial. Extracts most of its water from food.

Diet: Mainly eats small herbaceous plants and browses leaves, flowers, seeds, berries and fruits. Occasionally grazes, especially early in the wet season when grasses are most nutritious.

Numerous and regularly seen in Kruger, this small brownish antelope is told from other small antelope by its white belly and striking black-and-white patterning on the inside of the ears. It is believed to form monogamous pairs, with the individuals often foraging separately but using the same territorial dung piles, and making common urination displays. Breeding occurs year-round. Gestation is 170 days and the single calf is hidden in undergrowth and nursed for a few weeks before joining its parents; it becomes independent by three months. The main predators are Leopards, Caracals, jackals, Martial Eagles and Southern African Pythons.

To avoid detection Steenbok will remain motionless when a predator appears – but if this strategy fails will dart off with a zig-zag action and sometimes hide in a burrow or hole.

Steenbok have sleek, two-tone coats and distinctive strongly patterned ears.

Male

Female

☐ **Klipspringer** *Oreotragus oreotragus*

Size: HB 82–100 cm; Tail 6·5–10·3 cm

Weight: ♂ 9·1–11·6 kg, ♀ 10·5–15·9 kg

Key identification features: Small antelope with golden-brown coat grizzled with black hairs. Underparts pale; tail short. Head and muzzle triangular-shaped. Stands tall on hoof tips. Only male has short, straight, black horns approx. 10–13 cm in length.

Habitat: Highly specialized inhabitant of rocky outcrops, kopjes, gorges and escarpments.

Habits: Diurnal and crepuscular. Pairs occupy territories, but singletons and small groups associate. Often conspicuous, standing on top of exposed rocks, and running across open rocky terrain with a jerky gait.

Diet: Predominantly browses leaves, berries, fruits, seed pods and flowers; rarely eats grass.

This small brown antelope is uncommon and local in Kruger. It occurs in rocky places, unlike other antelope, and can be told by its triangular-shaped head. It has unique hollow, flattened hairs that insulate the body from extreme heat and cold. Klipspringers defend territories by visual displays, scent-marking (using a liquid secreted from glands below their eyes), and dung heap formation. Males will also fight with intruders. They breed year-round – a single calf being hidden and nursed for two months before leaving with its mother; calves are weaned after 4–5 months. Klipspringers are very agile and have specially adapted feet – the hooves are softer than those of most other antelope and provide a good purchase on rock surfaces, allowing them to walk and even run on near-vertical cliffs. Even so, they still occasionally fall prey to Leopards, Caracals and eagles.

Male

Female

☐ **Southern Reedbuck** *Redunca arundinum*
(Common Reedbuck)

Most easily seen around Pretoriuskop, this medium-sized, deer-like antelope is scarce in Kruger, with numbers estimated at around 300 individuals. It is only likely to be confused with Mountain Reedbuck (see *Key Identification Features*). Reedbucks are usually seen alone or in pairs, but occasionally associate in larger groups at the end of the breeding season or when food is locally abundant. Males, especially older individuals, defend territories to gain access to females, which they follow and test for sexual receptivity. Upon encountering a dominant male, subordinate males and females perform elaborate 'appeasement dances', involving spring-hop jumps with the tail curled-up. Each jump compacts air in a space in the groin that contains scent glands. As the reedbuck bounces, scented air is squeezed from the pocket making a popping noise. Reproduction occurs year-round, but most mating takes place early in the dry season. Births occur after a 230-day gestation, once the rains have set in from December to April. The single calf is hidden in tall cover for six weeks, with the mother returning periodically to suckle. Thereafter, the youngster joins its mother until it is weaned at 11–12 months. Females appear to locate their young by smell, and will defend them against predators by charging aggressively. All the larger predators will take Southern Reedbuck, which relies on camouflage to avoid detection.

Size: HB ♂ 130–160 cm, ♀ 120–140 cm; Tail 18–30 cm

Weight: ♂ 51–95 kg, ♀ 39–85 kg

Key identification features: Medium-sized, rusty-fawn antelope with a bushy tail and whitish underparts, small pointed ears and a black glandular patch beneath the eye and ear. Told from **Mountain Reedbuck** *Redunca fulvorufula* (rare in Kruger; not illustrated) by longer horns in male, less contrasting belly, and dark stripes on the front of the forelegs. Only the male has horns, which are 35–45 cm in length, splayed and curve forward.

Habitat: Tall grassy savannahs, and grassland, adjacent to permanent water. Avoids drier bush.

Habits: Active day and night, feeding at dawn and dusk. Occurs singly, in pairs, or small groups; no strong long-term bonds.

Diet: Grazes grass, including many species unpalatable to other ungulates, but occasionally browses herbs, leaves and shoots.

The Southern Reedbuck has the most deer-like appearance of Kruger's antelopes.

The male (*below*) is larger than the female (*above*) and has forward-curving horns.
The dark patches on the front of the forelegs are characteristic, and a good way of telling the
Southern Reedbuck from all other antelope in Kruger.

☐ **Bushbuck** *Tragelaphus scriptus*

The Bushbuck is a medium-sized antelope which is fairly common in Kruger, with numbers estimated at over 500 individuals. It is easily seen in certain rest camps in southern and central Kruger, such as Letaba where there are approachable individuals. Males have small, overlapping home ranges, but tend to avoid one another and are mostly solitary. The main social interactions are essentially between the sexes during mating and between mother and calf. The Bushbuck's social structure is thought to be to be a primitive, non-territorial arrangement in which the more dominant males mate with as many females as possible. Dominant males will posture and indulge in low-level aggression for mating rights, occasionally engaging in serious conflict. Dominant males also mate-guard females in breeding condition, although females may stray and copulate with younger males nearby. After a gestation of six months, a single calf is born in a secluded location, where it is nursed for four months before joining its mother. Although Bushbuck mate year-round, there is a peak in births during the wet season.

Size: HB ♂ 117–145 cm, ♀ 114–132 cm; Tail 19–24 cm

Weight: ♂ 40–80 kg, ♀ 24–60 kg

Key identification features: Adult male is mostly dark brown; female reddish-brown, both with variable white markings including 0–9 white vertical stripes. Only adult male has horns, approx. 30 cm in length. Nyala (*page 114*) is larger with 8–18 bold white vertical stripes. Bushbuck male lacks male Nyala's tawny 'socks' and long fringe that hangs between the throat and belly. Female Bushbuck has a whitish (not plain) throat.

Habitat: Riverine forest, thicket.

Habits: Mostly nocturnal and crepuscular; rests and ruminates during the day. Solitary or in pairs.

Diet: Chiefly browsers, with over 20 species of plant recorded in the diet.

A mature male

BUSHBUCK FAMILY TREE
Recent studies suggest that Bushbuck populations across Africa probably comprise several species, with some populations being more closely related to Bongo *Tragelaphus eurycerus* or Sitatunga *T. spekii* than they are to other Bushbuck. The animals in Kruger are sometimes referred to as the Imbabala and given the scientific name *T. sylvaticus*.

Young and female Bushbuck (*above*) are mainly reddish-brown, while males (*below*) become darker with age.

☐ Nyala *Tragelaphus angasii*

Size: HB ♂ 159–198 cm, ♀ 132–146 cm; Tail 34–47 cm

Weight: ♂ 92–126 kg, ♀ 55–68 kg

Key identification features: Adult male and female look very different. Male is dark grey-brown with 8–14 vertical white body stripes, tawny lower half to legs and long, shaggy hair hanging from the throat and belly. Female resembles female Bushbuck (*page 112*), but has up to 18 bold, vertical body stripes and often a black-tipped tail. Both sexes are larger than their Bushbuck counterparts. Only male has horns, approx. 70 cm in length, which have pale tips.

Habitat: Favours riverine forest, and thicket.

Habits: Active during day and night. Females and young form small groups, the membership of which is fluid. Older males are typically solitary. Not territorial.

Diet: Generalist browser on leaves, buds, fruits and flowers of many different species. More herbaceous vegetation and grass is eaten in the wet season.

Large, striking and beautiful, the Nyala is a scarce antelope estimated to number only around 300 individuals in Kruger. Despite its rarity, it is frequently encountered around Pafuri, in the far north of the park. It is readily identified by the vertical white stripes on the body. The Nyala may warrant its own genus, having diverged from other spiral-horned antelopes some eight million years ago.

Nyala occur in the same habitats as the smaller but superficially similar Bushbuck and is usually the dominant species.

As well as looking very different, male and female Nyalas have several ecological differences. The large males require a high calorific intake and select tall, woody vegetation, while the smaller females browse lower down, favouring herbaceous plants. Although Nyalas can survive extended periods without water, they do drink when the opportunity arises. Mating peaks during spring and autumn, with males competing fiercely for receptive females – posturing by raising the hairs along their back as a crest and lowering their head, and indulging in fights and scuffles. After a gestation of around seven months, a single calf is born in a thicket; the mother returns to tend the youngster for around 20 days before it joins her. The main predators are Leopards, Lions and African Wild Dogs, although baboons and large raptors will take young animals.

Male Nyala take about four years to reach maturity; in the meantime they look like females, but with developing horns.

This antelope gets its name from the Zulu moniker *'inyala'*; adult male (*below*) and female (*above*).

Roan Antelope *Hippotragus equinus*

Size: HB 200–219 cm; Tail 60–75 cm

Weight: ♂ 235–300 kg, ♀ 215–280 kg

Key identification features: Large, horse-like antelope; mostly fawn-coloured, with a boldly patterned black-and-white face. Both sexes have backward-arching, scimitar-like horns. Long, black-tipped ears extend sideways. Short, brush-like mane stops behind the shoulders. Short tail with black-tufted tip.

Habitat: Wooded habitat, preferring moist savannah with long grass and dense canopy.

Habits: Mostly diurnal, but will graze nocturnally in the heat of the wet season. Rests at midday. Drinks frequently. Small to large herds of females and young aggregate. Dominant males are more solitary and territorial, and subordinate males form bachelor groups.

Diet: Tall grasses, favouring the higher parts. Eats shrubs when grazing is poor.

Roan Antelopes form a crèche and the young remain close to the adults for protection.

The population of this large antelope has crashed dramatically in Kruger in recent years, probably due to predation and drought, and currently numbers only about 100 individuals. It is now a red-letter day to see a Roan Antelope and, with such a tiny population remaining, careful management will be required if the species is to persist. It is only likely to be confused with the Sable Antelope (*page 118*), but is paler brown and has shorter horns.

Herds of female Roan Antelopes roam widely, traversing the territories of several males. There is a clear hierarchy, with a dominant cow leading the herd, although challenges for her position occur frequently, accompanied by arched-neck displays. Young males form bachelor herds until they are about six years old, when they attempt to establish their own territories. Dominant males mark their territories with dung and defend any female herds entering the core area. Other males are seen off by pushing with horns, and tail lashing displays. Dominant males associate with female herds, testing regularly by smell

to determine whether any are sexually receptive; a female indicates her willingness to mate through submissive gestures. Breeding is non-seasonal and gestation lasts about nine months. Females separate from the herd to give birth and remain with the calf for the first week, thereafter leaving it alone, returning only periodically to feed it. After 4–5 weeks the calf joins the herd, and is weaned at six months.

The Roan Antelope's main predators are Spotted Hyenas, Leopards and African Wild Dogs but they are able to defend themselves using their sharp horns, and have been known to kill their hunters. Roan Antelopes have an unusual series of vocalizations: a high-pitched squeal when irritated, a snort when alarmed, and a hiss when injured.

Count your lucky stars if you see a Roan Antelope, as they are now very rare in Kruger. The Shingwedzi area is the hotspot for sightings.

The male (*right*) is larger, has a darker face and thicker, longer horns than the female (*left*).

☐ **Sable Antelope** *Hippotragus niger*

This large, stately antelope is scarce in Kruger, with a population of around 290 individuals, mostly in the northern half of the park. It may be confused with the Roan Antelope, but is darker brown and has longer horns.

Sable Antelopes are generally seen in herds, the size of which increases when it is dry and decreases when grazing is good during the wet season. They prefer to graze around termite mounds or drainage lines where the vegetation is lush, thereby avoiding competition with Plains Zebras and other grazers that favour shorter swards, and obtain essential minerals from salt licks and by chewing bones. The herd follows the dominant female, typically the oldest, and generally grazes an area intensively before moving on. Dominant males command a territory with almost constant contact with female herds, patrolling and marking the boundary by defecating, pawing the ground and beating the vegetation. They will follow any female herds that enter their territory, and even try to prevent them from leaving. Bulls will challenge each other for access to females, and display with tail raised, head erect and chin pulled in to impress the females. Gestation lasts almost nine months and calves remain hidden in dense bush for three weeks after birth before joining the herd, the mother returning periodically to care for them. Young females remain with the herd, but adolescent males are banished when about three years old and join bachelor groups, leaving when mature to become solitary and territorial. The main predators are Leopards, Lions, Spotted Hyenas and African Wild Dogs, although the formidable horns have inflicted mortal wounds on many an attacker.

Size: HB 185–194 cm; Tail 44–53 cm

Weight: ♂ 180–230 kg, ♀ 160–180 kg

Key identification features: Large, robust, horse-like antelope. Adult male and female look different. Male mostly blackish, with white belly and a boldly black-and-white patterned face and reddish-brown backs to the ears. Female more chestnut to reddish. Both sexes have backward-arching, scimitar-like horns, 50% longer than those of Roan Antelope (*page 116*).

Habitat: Broadleaved woodland, especially Mopane.

Habits: Mostly active at dawn and dusk, but into the night during hot conditions. Rests around midday. Females with young in herds of 15–25; males territorial and mostly solitary.

Diet: Prefers new green grass shoots that are longer than 20 cm. May eat leafy herbs and shrubs in the dry season.

Young Sable Antelope are reddish brown, like the female.

The male (*below*) is larger, darker and has longer more swept-back horns than the female (*above*).

☐ **Waterbuck** *Kobus ellipsiprymnus*

Size: HB 175–235 cm; Tail 33–44 cm

Weight: ♂ 250–275 kg, ♀ 160–180 kg

Key identification features: Sturdy antelope with shaggy, grizzled, grey-brown, long-haired coat, and white throat and facial markings. A diagnostic white circle around the buttocks and above the tail is unique. Only the male has horns, which are splayed and ridged, approx. 85 cm in length.

Habitat: Open grassland, wooded savannah and woodland, often close to water. Marshes and other wetlands.

Habits: Diurnal. Prefers to be active at dawn and dusk, resting and ruminating at midday. Females and young in small, loose groups. Dominant males are solitary and young males form bachelor groups.

Diet: Favours grasses and herbs, but eats reeds, sedges and browse in the dry season.

The Waterbuck is a large, thickset antelope which is common in Kruger, with numbers estimated at around 5,000 individuals. It is best told by the white ring around the buttocks.

Waterbucks produce an oily secretion from their skin that coats the fur; this is water resistant but also smelly and very distasteful and possibly acts to deter predators. This species' social structure is adaptable and flexible, females and young associating in herds that vary considerably in size and composition. Group size is smallest during the rainy season when perennial grasses are plentiful, sometimes numbering fewer than ten individuals, and highest in the dry season. Animals join different groups on a daily basis, and there is no defined leader or hierarchy in the female herds. However, young, subdominant males in bachelor groups have a strong hierarchy, reinforced by sparring. At maturity, dominant males obtain a territory through a variety

The Waterbuck has a white rump ring that looks as though it has sat on a painted toilet seat!

of display postures; physical conflict, including locking of horns, normally only arises when there is a serious challenge for territorial ownership. Males defend food resources in order to attract females into their territory. Reproduction occurs year-round, the male defending a female in breeding condition and regularly sniffing to test her readiness for copulation. Gestation lasts 240 days and a single calf is born; the youngster is nursed in isolation for 2–3 weeks before joining the herd.

There is considerable variation between Waterbuck, some individuals being very dark with a white throat patch.

The male is easily told from the female by its large horns.

Impala *Aepyceros melampus*

Size: HB ♂ 130–135 cm, ♀ 125–130 cm; Tail 25–30 cm

Weight: ♂ 57–60 kg, ♀ 43–47 kg

Key identification features: Tall and sleek. Fawn-brown with a paler tan panel along the flanks and a white belly and throat. Black stripe on each buttock and dark centre of the tail give a diagnostic 'M' pattern when viewed from the rear. Only male has horns, which are 42–92 cm long and lyre-shaped.

Habitat: Wooded savannah; scarce in forest and open grasslands.

Habits: Mostly diurnal. Males compete for territories, subordinate males form bachelor herds and females form groups with youngsters.

Diet: Highly adaptable, exploiting both grazing and browse. In the wet season they select the high quality leafy portion of grasses; in the dry season they shift to browsing shrubs, fruits and seeds.

The tall and elegant Impala is the commonest antelope in Kruger, numbering over 150,000 individuals. It is told from other antelope by its brown coloration and black markings on the rump and head.

Impala society is complex and changes with the seasons. In the wet season there are three main types of association: individual territorial males; bachelor herds; and female herds. Individual territorial males use urine and faeces, as well as scent glands at the base of their feet and sebaceous glands in their foreheads, to rub trees and tree stumps to mark their territories. Bachelor male herds comprise 25–40 individuals and

PERFECTLY ADAPTED

Scientists once thought the Impala was closely related to hartebeests and wildebeests but recent studies indicate that it diverged from other antelope 14 million years ago. It has distinctive features, such as a toothcomb on the front lower jaw that is used for grooming, and as a result is often placed in its own subfamily. Unchanged for the last five million years, the Impala has long been perfectly adapted to its environment.

female herds 15–100. Late in the wet season the breeding season or 'rut' begins. Testosterone levels are high, and territorial males become aggressive, emitting a musky odour. They reduce feeding in order to focus on breeding and territorial defence. The female herds shift between territorial males, which try to keep them in the centre of their territory. Males test females for receptivity by smell, chasing them around energetically if they are in breeding condition. Territoriality breaks down after the rut and dominant males may associate with bachelor herds. After a 180-day gestation a single calf is born and nursed in isolation for a few weeks before joining a nursery group close to the female herd. During the dry season, when food quality is poor, Impalas spend more time foraging and ruminating; their microbial gut fauna changing to enable them to digest less nutritious food.

Although almost all large predators will take Impala, they are particularly favoured by Leopards, Cheetahs and African Wild Dogs. Impala can jump incredibly high (up to 3 m) and daring launches are part of their 'flight response'. Another response to threats is to bury themselves in deep cover.

The male (*above*) has horns, while the female (*below*) does not.

☐ **Tsessebe** *Damaliscus lunatus*
(Topi)

Size: HB ♂ 207–229 cm, ♀ 190–226 cm; Tail approx. 45 cm

Weight: ♂ 140 kg, ♀ 126 kg

Key identification features: Odd-looking, narrow-faced antelope with dark blue-black and chestnut-brown fur. Legs tan-coloured below the knee. The 25–40 cm long horns splay outwards and recurve.

Habitat: Grassland in scattered woodland near permanent water. During the wet season roams more widely to exploit flushes of grass growth and temporary water.

Habits: Gregarious, with dominant territorial males maintaining 'harems' of females, and separate bachelor herds.

Diet: Grass, favouring growing leaves. Partial to re-sprouting post-burn patches.

This large brown antelope is rare in Kruger, with a population estimated at around 200 individuals. Within Kruger, it is told from similar antelope by the dark patches on the upper half of the legs and darker face.

Larger-horned male Tsessebes are most likely to be dominant, and mark their territory by pawing and scraping the ground, and by smearing grass stems with a sticky secretion exuded from a gland in front of each eye and glands on their feet. They will also rub their heads on the ground; the physical abrasion of the soil, and scent marking from facial glands perhaps serving to warn other males that they are entering a competitor's territory. Territorial males will also advertise their presence to potential competitors by standing broadside on a slightly raised mound. They will chase challengers, clash

horns, and fight if necessary, but this is unusual. The male retains a harem year-round and expels any male offspring when they are a year old. These form bachelor groups which often linger on the edge of the dominant male's territory. Tsessebes are seasonal breeders, with the rut taking place from January to March, and most births occurring from October to December. Unlike most other antelopes in Kruger the calves are not hidden, and join and follow the herd immediately after birth.

The Tsessebe is one of the fastest antelopes in the world, capable of reaching a speed of 80 km/h and maintaining this for quite a distance; it is therefore a difficult quarry for predators to catch.

The Tsessebe has a very long face with dark patches – and when seen from the front the tips of the horns curve inwards.

Common Wildebeest *Connochaetes taurinus*
(Blue Wildebeest; White-bearded Wildebeest; Gnu)

Size: HB 170–240 cm; Tail 60–100 cm

Weight: ♂ 232–295 kg, ♀ 164–216 kg

Key identification features:
Front-heavy, muscular antelope. Broad, flat forehead and muzzle; sideways-recurved, bull-like horns (longer in male) form a boss; bearded tassels hang from chin and throat; shoulders are higher than the hips. Body colour is blue-brown on a short, shiny, velvet coat, with darker vertical stripes.

Habitat: Savannah and woodland with short grass.

Habits: Every 24-hour cycle, some eight hours are spent eating, mostly during the day, but also at night. Needs to drink daily. Groups consist of territorial males, female herds and bachelor groups.

Diet: Grazer, preferring short, lush grass 10–15 cm high. Partial to areas with post-burn regrowth. During the dry season will switch to other plant species.

GNU NAMES
The Common Wildebeest's generic scientific name *Connochaetes* is derived from the Greek *kónnos*, meaning beard, and *khaítē* meaning mane, describing the animal's flowing facial locks. Southern Africa's original inhabitants, the Khoikhoi people, called them 'Gnu', an onomatopoeic name reflecting their most common sound – a name that is widely used even to this day.

This large brown antelope is common in Kruger, with numbers estimated at more than 12,000 individuals. It has a distinctive shape, with bulky forequarters and slimmer, lower hindquarters.

Dominant males hold small, fixed territories, where they often remain even when females move to areas with better grazing. Territories are marked using secretions from a gland in front of each eye, which is rubbed on the ground, bushes or tree trunks. Bulls fight by clashing heads and bashing their bosses together. Territorial males will attempt to keep

females within their territory by swishing their tails and lowering their heads. In Kruger, the seasonal breeding rut lasts from April to June, during which time males become more frisky, aggressive and territorial; females move between territories, mating with more than one male. After a gestation of just over eight months a single calf is born. Within minutes it gets to its feet and joins its mother, thereafter remaining with the herd. The young are tawny-brown and playful, taking on adult traits at about two months of age. Wildebeest are skittish, and will bolt at the first sign of danger, bounding away and tossing their heads in the direction of the threat. Although appearing clumsy, they are surprisingly fast and able to reach speeds of 75 km/h. Wildebeest are preyed upon by Lions, Spotted Hyenas and African Wild Dogs, and the young are taken by Leopards and Cheetahs.

A calf must be able to stand within minutes of being born so that it can remain with the herd.

◼ Scrub Hare *Lepus saxatilis*

Size: HB 45–64 cm; Tail 7–12 cm

Weight: 1·5–3·5 kg (♀ heavier than ♂)

Key identification features: Grizzled grey-black upperparts and white underparts. Lighter fur on face and around eyes. Often has a rusty coloured collar but this is only seen if the head is extended and ears raised.

Habitat: Scrubby grasslands in savannah.

Habits: Nocturnal, rarely seen by day. Solitary.

Diet: Grass, leaves, stems and rhizomes.

The Scrub Hare is frequently seen on night drives. The African Savannah Hare *Lepus microtis* (not illustrated) is also thought to occur in Kruger but since the two species are impossible to separate in the field, the status of the African Savannah Hare is unclear. Hares are most active on warm and dry evenings, sheltering in scrub and bushes by day. They escape predation by 'freezing' before suddenly running off in a characteristic zigzag pattern. Hares do not have social bonds and will breed with many partners year-round (even when there is severe drought), although births peak during the wet season. After a gestation of 42 days, 1–3 young (leverets) are born (fully haired, and with their eyes open). Hares do not invest much effort in parenting, and after suckling for a few days the young are expelled and go their own way.

■ Springhare *Pedetes capensis*
(Spring Hare)

Size: HB 34–42 cm; Tail 35–49 cm	

Weight: 2·5–3·8 kg

Key identification features: Strange mini kangaroo-like creature. Sits upright on large hind legs with forelegs held outstretched like a horse-rider. Bounds on hind legs in a unique manner for an African mammal. Body is tawny above, whitish underneath. Has a rather square face, rabbit-like ears 7 cm in length, and a long buff-and-black tail.

Habitat: Sandy plains, pans, areas with loose, dry soil, often close to rivers.

Habits: Strictly nocturnal. Excavates and lives in burrows, moving between them regularly. Territorial.

Diet: Mainly herbivorous, digging for foliage, roots and other vegetable matter, and sometimes insects.

Despite its name, the distinctive Springhare, with its long hind legs and

KANGAROO CONVERGENCE
Like Australasia's famous kangaroos, the springhares live on low-energy resources. They have both evolved a hopping gait that allows them to move quickly and with minimal effort, thereby preserving their energy.

tail, is not a hare at all, but a rodent. Even so, it has no close relatives and is placed in its own unique family (Pedetidae). Springhares are uncommon in Kruger but sometimes encountered on night drives. They dig burrows up to 50 m in length, fleeing to them at any sign of danger. They breed year-round, producing young 3–4 times annually. After an 80-day gestation, a single pup is born; it is covered in hair and opens its eyes after three days – an unusually rapid rate of development for a rodent. The youngster first leaves the burrow when it is half-grown at about seven weeks of age. Springhares are subject to predation by pythons, eagle-owls and nocturnal mammalian predators.

☐ **Rock Hyrax** *Procavia capensis*
(Rock Dassie)

Size: TL 38–60 cm

Weight: 1·8–5 kg

Key identification features: Rabbit-sized, but looks like a giant, tail-less Guinea Pig *Cavia porcellus*: woolly and brown, with a pointed muzzle, short neck and small, rounded ears.

Habitat: Rocks, cliffs, occasionally trees.

Habits: Diurnal. Colonies of 10–80 dominated by one male with many females occupy rocky crevices, where they live and hide, but emerge to sunbathe and call.

Diet: Mostly grasses and herbs, but may also browse on shrubs.

This odd, rodent-like animal is fairly common on rocky outcrops in Kruger. It has tusk-like incisors that are used for grooming and defence, and disproportionately large jaws with strong molars adapted for chewing large mouthfuls of food. Hyraxes have multi-chambered stomachs containing bacteria that assist in digesting tough plant material.

They are also able to control water loss, producing thick and syrupy urine when the conditions are dry. Hyraxes emit loud territorial calls, including wailing and snorting, which combine about 30 syllables: similar vocal repertoires in other mammals, may have been a precursor to more complex vocal communication.

IT'S ALL RELATIVE
Although elephants are often cited as being the closest relatives to the hyraxes, the manatees *Trichechus* spp. and Dugong *Dugong dugon* are in fact also equal cousins. Hyraxes diverged from these other groups some 60 million years ago, and are an isolated lineage.

HYRAXES IN THE SHADOWS
Hyraxes were among the most dominant herbivores of the African bush 30–25 million years ago, and some species were large. However, as the ungulates rose to claim that mantle, hyraxes declined and retreated to marginal habitats.

SWEATY FEET
A hyrax's sweat glands are on its feet; their function is to moisten the soft footpads and increase grip on smooth rock surfaces, rather than providing a cooling mechanism.

Size: HB 75–100 cm; Tail 10–17 cm	

Weight: 10–24 kg

Key identification features: Very large, dark rodent with white-tipped neck crest and unique hardened black-and-white banded quills, and whitish rump. Ponderous shuffling gait can be converted into a run when required.

Habitat: Almost anywhere, but prefers rocky terrain with crevices in which they can hide.

Habits: Nocturnal. Monogamous. Males, females and young live in family groups, but often forage alone.

Diet: Herbivore. Digs for roots, bulbs and tubers; also eats bark and fallen fruits. Gnaws on bones for additional nutrients.

This large and distinctive rodent is common in Kruger, but is nocturnal and seldom seen. Porcupines are covered in hard, pliable spines and sharp quills that are used for protection. The animal can appear to double its size by erecting the quills, and shakes them to create an intimidating rattling sound. When threatened, a Cape Porcupine will present its rear end and sprint backwards to lodge the erected quills into the face of its attacker; Lions and Leopards have died from septicaemia associated with the resulting wounds. Porcupines have a habit of killing trees by ring-barking them, and appear to play an important role in altering the composition of habitats.

☐ **Vervet (Monkey)** *Chlorocebus pygerythrus*

Size: HB ♂ 50–65 cm, ♀ 38–62 cm;
Tail 48–75 cm

Weight: ♂ 3·9–8·0 kg, ♀ 3·5–5·0 kg

Key identification features: Brown-grey upperparts, paler belly and chest, and black face, tail-tip, hands and feet. Male has sky-blue scrotum and red penis.

Habitat: Savannah; favours riverine forest along drainage lines. Avoids open areas.

Habits: Diurnal. Very sociable in groups of 10–50.

Diet: Mostly vegetarian: fruits, flowers, tree gum and seeds, but occasionally invertebrates and birds' eggs.

The Vervet is the most common and widespread monkey in Kruger, living in large troops with a complex social structure. Males move to new troops when they mature, but females remain within their maternal troop. The sexes have different dominance hierarchies: the status of males is based on their age, fighting ability and the status of their allies; while that of females tends to be passed down from mothers to daughters, with high-ranking mothers tending to have high-ranking daughters. An individual's overall status depends both on its particular position within a clan, and that clan's status relative to other clans.

Vervets have a complicated vocal communication system that includes three distinct alarm calls, each of which elicits different responses based on the type of predator concerned. The 'predatory bird' alarm will have all the monkeys scanning the sky, the 'snake' alarm results in them surveying the ground, and the 'cat' alarm will have them scattering into the trees. In addition, individual Vervets can distinguish the different voices of other group members.

The behaviour of Vervets is fascinating and the subject of much conjecture.

Young Vervets remain extremely close to their mothers, and are lavished with attention and care.

For example, some individuals have been observed to destroy the food of another troop member, rather than eat it themselves – thought, perhaps, to improve the individual's own social standing in the troop. Another interesting behaviour is surrogate mothering. Baby Vervets are the focus of considerable group attention, and much of the care is undertaken by young females that have yet to become sexually mature. These females preferentially choose to look after the young of high-ranking, closely related females, as doing so allows them to improve their own social standing and gain parenting experience. Mothers prefer to use their own daughters as surrogate mothers, thereby imparting skills to their own offspring. Once the young are being nurtured by a surrogate mother (or mothers) the female is able to breed again.

The male Vervet is larger than the female and has a colourful blue scrotum and red penis. When confronting competing groups, males will stand up in a ritualized display, exposing their genitals.

☐ **Chacma Baboon** *Papio ursinus*

Size: HB ♂ 68–100 cm, ♀ 51–62 cm;
Tail 37–84 cm

Weight: ♂ 25–35 kg, ♀ 12–20 kg

Key identification features: Large; uniformly grey-brown with blackish, naked face. Fused vertebrae make the tail appear 'kinked'. Male has long, angular, dog-like snout and huge canine teeth, and is twice the size of a female.

Habitat: Virtually anywhere, provided there is access to permanent water.

Habits: Diurnal. Mostly terrestrial, moving on the ground on all-fours; will also occupy trees or cliffs to forage, roost and evade predators.

Diet: Opportunistic omnivores, eating fruits, seeds, roots, invertebrates, birds' eggs and any larger vertebrate they can catch and kill.

The Chacma Baboon is a large brown monkey that is common and widespread in Kruger. It occurs in troops, which can number from 4–130 individuals, but average 40; these are governed by strict multi-male–multi-female dominance hierarchies. Males use their large canines and physical prowess to establish dominance, often making a loud "*wahoo*" call to proclaim their status, while females inherit their rank from their parents. Same-sex alliances are rare, and often the important relationships that determine dominance are between unrelated males and females. Troop members communicate through body language, facial expressions, vocalizations and touch.

If the dominant males in a troop are overthrown, the new males will often indulge in mass infanticide, killing any youngsters not sired by them. This results in the females coming quickly into breeding condition, providing an opportunity for the new dominant males to pass on their own genes. Females that are 4–5 years old, and not yet sexually mature, will sometimes 'adopt' orphaned babies. These individuals thereby gain experience for when they become mothers, or, if the adoptions are of related babies, the surrogate mothers ensure the survival of closely related family members.

MONKEY BUSINESS
The male's large canines are not just for intimidation, but also offer protection against predators and other threats. The Chacma Baboon's main enemies are Leopards, and they will often invest considerable effort into ejecting, or even killing, any Leopard in their territory.

BITING THE HAND THAT FEEDS
Never feed monkeys or baboons, no matter how 'cute' they look. This results in them becoming habitual beggars, and such a nuisance that they have to be eliminated by the park authorities.

n their own family, the galagos (or bushbabies) are an ancient lineage of primates that originated some 40–50 million years ago (MYA) and dominated their niche before the evolution of monkeys, which largely replaced them, around 30 MYA. Galagos are strictly nocturnal primates that roost in tree hollows during the day to avoid predators. Their large, globular eyes have many rod-cells packed into the retina, an adaptation that renders them red-green colour blind but enables excellent vision in low-light. Their night vision is further enhanced by a mirror-like layer behind the retina, which is why their eyes are so reflective. Galagos can move their large ears independently which enables them to detect small movements of invertebrate prey with great accuracy. Their elongated, spring-like hindlimbs mean they are excellent jumpers; with their long tails used as a counterbalance. They urinate on their hands in order to create scent-trails to mark their territories.

Southern Lesser Galago *Galago moholi*
(Lesser Bushbaby; South African Galago; Mohol Galago)

Size: HB 12–17 cm; Tail 16–28 cm

Weight: ♂ 160–255 g, ♀ 95–200 g

Key identification features: Tiny, squirrel-sized; silver-grey fur. Huge ears; large, forward-facing eyes. Short muzzle with a pale nose stripe; black diamond-shaped eye-rings; bulbous head gives it a 'cute' appearance. Fingers are padded and tail is long and thin with a fluffy tip.

Habitat: Thorn tree woodland, Mopane, and thickets; prefers drier country.

Habits: Nocturnal. Single male has multiple female mates. Leaps and bounds frequently, often sitting upright and clinging to smaller vertical branches.

Diet: Mostly invertebrates, tree gum, and occasionally fruits and seeds.

This small and agile lemur-like galago is fairly common in Kruger and occasionally seen in treetops or scurrying rapidly along branches at night. The fingers are covered with thickened skin which acts like sucker pads and allows them to grip onto smooth bark. The 1–2 young are born after a four-month gestation, and the mother transfers them between resting places by carrying them in her mouth; she does this for about six weeks until they become independent.

BUSHBABY RELATIONSHIPS
The closest relatives of galagos are the lemurs of Madagascar and the lorises and tarsiers of Asia. The relationships between Galago species is poorly understood, and the two species that occur in Kruger have several different names.

Thick-tailed Greater Galago *Otolemur crassicaudatus*
(Greater Bushbaby; Large-eared Greater Galago)

Size: HB 26–40 cm; Tail 30–40 cm

Weight: ♂ 1·1–1·8 kg, ♀ 1·2–1·5 kg

Key identification features: Large, cat-sized. Rounded ears; long, dog-like muzzle with large, forward-facing eyes; long, bushy tail. Thick, grey-brown fur and lobed, padded toes.

Habitat: Thickets and riverine forest.

Habits: Nocturnal. Generally moves by walking and running along branches in trees, but jumps well and occasionally moves on the ground.

Diet: Invertebrates, small vertebrates, fruits, tree gum and seeds.

This large, possum-like galago is fairly common in Kruger and occasionally seen on night drives or by searching in camps with a torch after dark. Although less agile than the Southern Lesser Galago, the Thick-tailed Greater Galago is still an accomplished jumper, capable of leaping over 2 m horizontally. Females make leafy nests to conceal their young (1–3, usually two) but they can still fall prey to Leopards, owls, snakes and genets.

CRY BABIES
Galagos get their alternative name of bushbaby from the strained, infant-like "*whaaaah*"cries that the larger species emit at night.

☐ Smith's Bush Squirrel *Paraxerus cepapi*
(Tree Squirrel)

Size: HB 16·6–19·1 cm; Tail 11·5–21·5 cm

Weight: 117–265 g

Key identification features: Kruger's only squirrel. Small and slender, grizzled, tawny with whitish belly. Narrow tail.

Habitat: Widespread in savannah, both in trees and on the ground though avoids forests. Prefers areas with a high density of holes for nesting, hiding and foraging.

Habits: Diurnal. Small groups of males and females associate.

Diet: Primarily vegetarian, feeding on flowers, leaves, seeds, berries, fruits and bark. Also eats insects, especially when other food is scarce.

This small squirrel is common and widespread in Kruger, and light and agile enough to be able to access food beyond the reach of most other mammals. When resources are abundant, they cache seeds and nuts for later consumption. They occur in family groups and reinforce their social bonds by mutual grooming using scent from their anal glands. Together, they vigorously defend their territory against other squirrels. Individuals also mob predators by emitting clicking noises and flicking their tails, but if threatened bolt to tree holes and hide. When a female is in breeding condition, she will be courted by the resident male as well as others nearby. Gestation takes 50–60 days and the 1–3 hairless babies are born in a nest, normally located in a tree crevice. The young are dependent upon their highly attentive mother for 20 days and stay with their parents until sexually mature at 6–9 months, at which point they are evicted and go their own way.

☐ Epauletted fruit-bats *Epomophorus* spp.

Size: TL ♂ 15 cm, ♀ 12 cm

Weight: ♂ 80–140 g, ♀ 64–88 g

Key identification features: Brown, large-eyed; dog-like snout. Obvious white patch at the base of each ear. Two species, **Wahlberg's Fruit-bat** *E. wahlbergi* and **Peters's Fruit-bat** *E. crypturus*, occur together at some camps and can only be separated in the hand (by detailed examination of the inside of their mouth).

Habitat: Riverine forest and large trees.

Habits: Nocturnal, flying, fruit-eater. Slightly nomadic, changing locality depending on fruit abundance. Gregarious: roosts of up to 100 by day in trees along rivers and in camps.

Diet: Soft pulpy fruit, especially figs and Marula.

Roosts of epauletted fruit-bats are fairly common in Kruger's camps. Once local fruit resources have been exhausted, the roost shifts closer to a fresh food source.

These large bats are fairly common and widespread in Kruger. They are told from the 40 or so other bat species recorded in the park (which are mostly small insect-eaters) by their size and the white tufts at the base of the ears. Despite the name, it is only the males that have epaulettes – a patch of white hair on each shoulder that covers a sunken glandular pouch. The epaulettes are only exposed on the rare occasion that the glandular pouch is inverted, which happens when the animal is under stress, vocalizing, or perhaps sexually stimulated. The male's call is a musical bark, a sound that betrays this animal's presence at night. After a gestation of around 5 months, females give birth to a single pup (rarely twins), which, while very young, clings to one of its mother's nipples and is carried by her while she is feeding.

Reptiles

The spectacular **Common Rough-scaled Lizard** *Meroles squamulosus* is one of around 118 reptile species in Kruger. This book features 17 species that are more likely to be found. Reptile watching can become addictive and if this book sparks an interest, get a more comprehensive resource on reptiles of southern Africa (see *Further reading, page 170*).

☐ **Nile Crocodile** *Crocodylus niloticus*

Size: TL ♂ 3·5–5·0 m (max. 5·9 m);
♀ 2·4–3·85 m

Weight: 225–550 kg (max. 1 tonne)
(♂ heavier than ♀)

Key identification features: Enormous, long, flat, short-legged reptile with many-toothed jaw, long snout with eyes set on top, and prominent elevated armoured horny plates on the back and tail. Olive-bronze in colour with paler belly.

Habitat: Rivers, pans, marshes, dams and other wetlands.

Habits: Aquatic. When not in the water likes to bask on shallow banks. Lies in ambush until prey is close, and then attacks with an incredible burst of speed.

Diet: Opportunistic, will take small and large mammals, fish, reptiles, birds and invertebrates.

The huge Nile Crocodile is common throughout Kruger wherever there are wetlands. The largest individuals can be monsters that live for 70–100 years. It is the second largest reptile on Earth, after the Saltwater Crocodile *Crocodylus porosus* of Southern Asia and Australia. Because of their flattened bodies and toothy grins, they are colloquially called 'flatdogs'.

This apex predator is a highly efficient hunter, making most attacks in the water (rarely on land) and seizing and drowning its prey in immensely powerful jaws. A Nile Crocodile can eat up to half its body weight in one meal, and then go for six months or more without eating. Crocodile hierarchies are determined by size, with the largest males dominating – occupying the best basking areas and defending food resources. To attract females, males bellow and blow water from their noses. About two months after mating, around 50 eggs are deposited in a nest that the female has dug in a dry, sandy riverbank. After covering the nest, the dedicated mother will guard it for some three months until the eggs hatch. The sex of the hatchlings is determined by the average temperature inside the nest during the middle-third of the incubation period: if 31·7°C–34·5°C they will be male; if above or below that temperature range they will be female. Upon hatching, the young emit clucking noises that alerts the mother who then excavates the nest and tenderly transfers the young in her mouth to the nearest sizeable waterbody. The young crocodiles are protected by their mother for two years, although many are lost to predation by monitors and terrapins.

It is unclear why crocodiles gape: some scientists have suggested it is to cool down, although this does not explain why they also gape in cold conditions. Any tooth that a crocodile loses is quickly replaced, and this may happen thousands of times during the animal's lifetime.

☐ Leopard Tortoise *Stigmochelys pardalis*

Size: TL 30–46 cm (max. 70 cm)

Weight: 8–20 kg

Key identification features: The only tortoise in Kruger larger than 20 cm. Carapace is high and domed, with pyramid-shaped plates (scutes) marked with rosettes similar to those of a leopard. Animals become darker with age.

Habitat: Varied, but requires access to good grass grazing.

Habits: Diurnal. Terrestrial. Solitary. Most active after rains and can become dormant for weeks at a time during the dry season.

Diet: Mainly herbivorous. Grasses and other vegetation; fruits. Gnaws bones and eats hyena faeces to obtain supplementary calcium.

The Leopard Tortoise is fairly common in south and central Kruger, but scarce in the north. **Bell's Hinged Tortoise** *Kinixys belliana* and **Speke's Hinged Tortoise** *K. spekii* (neither illustrated) also occur in Kruger but do not grow larger than 210 mm or weigh more than 2 kg. Leopard Tortoises live for 50–100 years in the wild; although only 40–50 mm in length when hatched, they grow fast and reach maturity in 12–15 years. Leopard Tortoises can move surprisingly fast and are able to climb rocky terrain. Males will engage in combat, pushing and butting one another in an attempt to overturn their opponent. Females bury their eggs in the ground and these take 10–15 months to incubate. If it is dry and the ground baked hard when the eggs hatch, the youngsters may have to wait weeks for the first rain before they are able to dig themselves out and make their way to freedom. Although young tortoises have many predators, adults are seldom killed, their greatest hazard being to crack their carapace as a result of falling.

■ Serrated Hinged Terrapin *Pelusios sinuatus*

Size: TL 30–40 cm

Weight: 4·5–7 kg (♀ heavier than ♂)

Key identification features: Large, dark, terrapin with serrated rear carapace. The well-domed, rounded shell, lack of a pale chin and throat, and weak bill with two tooth-like structures, distinguish this species from the smaller, more flattened, **Central Marsh Terrapin** *Pelomedusa subrufa* (not illustrated).

Habitat: Ponds, dams and rivers.

Habits: Aquatic. Basks on logs, banks or other surfaces and forages in the water.

Diet: Water snails, mussels, insects, vegetation and carrion.

This fairly large terrapin with a high-domed carapace is very common in wetlands throughout Kruger, and only likely to be confused with the **Central Marsh Terrapin** (not illustrated but see *Key identification features*). It lays about ten eggs in the ground within half a kilometre of water, and the hatchlings emerge towards the end of the wet season. During the dry season these terrapins may bury themselves in mud and enter a state of torpor (aestivation). When it rains they revive and disperse, when they can be found far from water. When threatened, the hinged shell can be closed to protect the head and front limbs, and the animal can secrete a noxious odour to repel predators.

When mammals visit waterholes to wallow, the Serrated Hinged Terrapin will sometimes take advantage of an easy meal by picking ticks off their skin.

MONITORS

Monitors are large and muscular lizards with sharp claws that are used to climb trees and river embankments, tear open nests of reptiles and birds or dig out prey. Their forked tongues have highly developed olfactory senses, allowing them to detect food, enemies or mates by smell. Females lay eggs in an excavated hole, sometimes inside an active termite mound, which maintains the perfect temperature and humidity and offers protection from predators. The young emerge 90 days later, although many nests are lost as a result of predation by mongooses. The two monitors that occur in Kruger can go into dry season torpor if necessary. Martial Eagles, pythons and crocodiles are the major predators.

☐ Rock Monitor *Varanus albigularis*

Size: TL 70–100 cm (max. 150 cm)

Weight: ♂ 6·1–8·0 kg, ♀ 3·2–5·0 kg

Key identification features – see opposite: Stout, strong lizard, shorter tailed and bulkier than Water Monitor. The base of the tail is cylindrical, sometimes flattening towards the tip. Tends to be browner than Water Monitor and often has a dark line (absent in Water Monitor) running from the eye to the neck over the ear openings; juvenile is more boldly marked, with black and yellow-brown patches and bands. When moving, head held level with the back.

Habitat: Broad range of savannah habitats.

Habits: Diurnal. Solitary. Lives in a burrow under a rock excavated by another animal, or occasionally in a tree hole. Plays dead when threatened.

Diet: Opportunistic, but prefers invertebrates. Scavenges on carrion.

☐ Water Monitor *Varanus niloticus*

Size: TL 150–180 cm (max. 244 cm)

Weight: 1·7–5·0 kg (max. 15 kg)

Key identification features – see opposite: Stout but lithe lizard with extremely long tail.
The tail is laterally flattened. More boldly marked than Rock Monitor, with bands of yellow spots down the back; juvenile is more strikingly black-and-yellow patterned. When moving, head held high – above the level of the back.

Habitat: Riverine woodland, pan and lake margins, sandbanks.

Habits: Diurnal, semi-aquatic and an excellent swimmer. Basks on outcrops or tree trunks.

Diet: Opportunistic, including fish, snails, crabs, frogs, terrapins, young crocodiles, birds, mammals, large insects and carrion.

THE EINSTEIN LIZARD
Monitors are surprisingly intelligent: in an experiment where they were offered different quantities of snails it was shown that they were able to count to six.

HEART RATE MONITOR
Monitors often remain motionless, and only when danger is very close will they tear off at high speed, making a considerable noise. This often leads to a major adrenalin rush for whatever animal was approaching, unaware of the monitor's presence.

Rock Monitor

Water Monitor

Monitors are best told apart by the shape of their snout and the position and shape of their nostrils.
Rock Monitor (*above*) has a bulbous snout with slit-like nostrils close to the eyes.
Water Monitor (*below*) has an elongated snout with rounded nostrils located towards the tip;

Juvenile

147

■ Puff Adder *Bitis arietans*

Size: TL 70–120 cm

Weight: 3–6 kg (♀ heavier than ♂)

Key identification features: Rather short, fat-bodied snake with triangular head and blunt snout. Colour pattern varies, but blotched brown-and-tan individuals with blackish chevrons are most frequent. Two oblique dark bars from the eyes to the lips are distinctive.

Habitat: Wide variety, but avoids forest. Usually terrestrial, but can climb.

Habits: Primarily nocturnal. This is a stealth hunter which lies motionless waiting for prey to venture close before launching an ambush. However, can move with speed if disturbed.

Diet: Small mammals, birds and lizards.

Although common, the cryptic and nocturnal Puff Adder is seldom seen in Kruger. When threatened, Puff Adders often inflate their bodies (hence their name) and hiss loudly. They are lethargic, relying on camouflage to catch their prey, but will strike in defence if accidently stood on. They have large, hinged fangs and inject a highly venomous cell-killing toxin that results in severe swelling. While human deaths from snakebites are rare in South Africa, a significant proportion of fatalities are attributable to the Puff Adder, reflecting the fact that this snake is so widespread and well camouflaged. Puff Adders give birth to usually 20–40 young, each encapsulated in a fine membrane from which they break out of almost immediately.

Mozambique Spitting Cobra *Naja mossambica* EXTREMELY VENOMOUS

Size: TL 90–120 cm	

Weight: 1–2 kg

Key identification features: Medium-large snake with a blunt head. Brownish above with black-edged scales giving a fishnet pattern. Throat and belly fawn-pink with irregular blotchy black cross-bands that are particularly noticeable when the snake rears up with its hood expanded.

Habitat: Savannah, particularly localities near water.

Habits: Primarily nocturnal. Skittish and nervous; when threatened will either feign death or rear up, fanning its hood. Swims readily.

Diet: Amphibians, birds, small mammals and other snakes.

SNAKEBITE SENSATIONALISM
Snakebites are extremely rare. Millions of tourists visit Kruger annually and most never even see a snake. The press often sensationalizes any incident, but the chances of having an unfortunate altercation with one of these beautiful and misunderstood creatures is remote.

The Mozambique Spitting Cobra is common, but secretive and seldom seen in Kruger. The rarer Snouted Cobra *Naja annulifera* (not illustrated) also occurs in Kruger but is larger and tends to be more mottled or banded, lacking the fawn-pink belly of Mozambique Spitting Cobra. The Mozambique Spitting Cobra is one of Africa's most dangerous snakes and when threatened can squirt its venom accurately up to three metres, specifically aiming at the aggressor's eyes, causing temporary damage. The venom is a cell-killing toxin, bites causing severe tissue destruction. Females lay a clutch of 10–20 eggs; these hatch after 60 days and the hatchlings measure about 240 mm.

Black Mamba *Dendroaspis polylepis*

EXTREMELY VENOMOUS

Size: TL 200–250 cm (max. 430 cm)

Weight: 1–2 kg

Key identification features: Large, long, streamlined snake, uniformly coloured olive or slaty with a coffin-shaped head, black eyes, and broad smiling mouth with a glossy blue-black lining (which gives this snake its name).

Habitat: Savannah, preferring drier scrub and rocky environments.

Habits: Diurnal. Prefers to remain on the ground, but capable climbers. Territorial, usually returning to a favoured lair such as an abandoned termite mound. Will strike when threatened.

Diet: Opportunistic; prefers mammals such as rodents and hyraxes but will also eat birds, reptiles (including other snakes) and insects and other invertebrates.

This large snake is common and regularly seen in Kruger, particularly during the wet season. It is active and capable of moving at speeds of up to 4 m/second and this, together with the fact that it has rapidly acting, highly toxic venom that attacks the nervous system, makes it a formidable hunter. Without anti-venom serum and quick action, serious tissue damage (and possibly death) is likely for anyone unfortunate enough to be bitten. Even so, this incredible snake has its own enemies, including snake-eagles, crocodiles, mongooses and, of course, humans.

MAMBA MAMBO
Probably due to their speed, dexterity and weaponry, mambas feature prominently in African mythology. Some stories attribute them with considerable intelligence, such as being able to plot an attack on humans. There are also legends that include mambas holding the tail in their mouth, and rolling downhill like a bicycle tyre, before straightening their body into a missile to strike at speed.

☐ Southern African Python *Python natalensis*

Size: TL 300–500 cm

Weight: 44–55 kg (♀ heavier than ♂)

Key identification features: A thick, muscular snake with a large, triangular head. Olive and brown with dappled darker blotches, giving it disruptive camouflage. Two pale stripes run from the nostrils to the back of the head creating a distinctive dark arrow-shaped wedge on the crown. The underside is pale. Large teeth.

Habitat: A wide variety of savannah, often close to water or rocky areas.

Habits: Nocturnal and crepuscular, foraging at dawn and dusk. Regularly basks in the sun at midday.

Diet: Small and large mammals, crocodiles, fish and monitor lizards.

Common and regularly seen in Kruger, this huge, placid snake (one of Africa's largest) is non-venomous, but when provoked may occasionally bite, leading to secondary infections. Pythons are ambush hunters that kill by coiling themselves around the victim's body and squeezing it to death before swallowing it. They take prey as large as antelopes and crocodiles, and have scales on their lips with heat-sensitive pits that are used to detect warm-blooded animals. The female protects the eggs and hatchlings, showing a surprising level of parental care for a snake. Pythons may be attacked by Lions, Spotted Hyenas, African Wild Dogs or Honey Badgers, being especially vulnerable if they have recently swallowed large prey and, as a consequence, are unable to move.

☐ Common Flap-necked Chameleon *Chamaeleo dilepis*

Size: TL 35–40 cm (♂ smaller than ♀)

Key identification features: Kruger's only chameleon. Large, with a ridge of small spines running down the throat and belly; small neck flaps. The colour changes depending on its mood and other environmental factors, but it is usually green, brown or yellow. Male has a hind foot spur, which female lacks.

Habitat: Diurnal. Arboreal in wooded savannah, but also moves on the ground.

Habits: Solitary; female only allows male to approach for mating.

Diet: Insects and other invertebrates.

Although this strange lizard is common and often seen in Kruger, it is most easily found at night, when it sleeps with its tail coiled and turns a conspicuous ghostly whitish colour. A chameleon's eyes are located within rotatable turrets and move independently. This gives the animal 360-degree vision and the ability to track an approaching object whilst at the same time scanning its surroundings. Once prey is located, both eyes focus on it, enabling the chameleon to judge the distance. Prey is captured using a long, sticky tongue that is extended at incredible speed. Chameleons move slowly and with a rocking motion, possibly mimicking waving leaves – either to break up their outline and avoid predation, or perhaps enabling them to get closer to their prey. Eggs are buried in a hole in the ground and hatch nine months later; the young then take some 12 months to mature. Uniquely, chameleons adjust a layer of special cells in their skin to change colour. This reptile's defence strategy involves turning black, hissing, inflating the body and opening the mouth, and even resorting to biting. Despite this, they still often fall prey to monkeys, snakes and birds.

KARMA CHAMELEON
Chameleons are much feared by superstitious local people, who will deliberately drive over them if they are seen crossing roads. They are regarded as harbingers of death, and practitioners of witchcraft, with a deadly bite – all of which is, of course, entirely false.

☐ Southern Tree Agama
Acanthocercus atricollis

Adult males bob their unmistakable head during display.

Size: TL 20–30 cm (♂ larger than ♀)

Key identification features: Large and broad-headed. Ear opening is larger than the eye. Adult male unmistakable with a blue head and yellow-orange back. Female and sub-adult male are both cryptic olive-brown with black shoulder spots. The tail is banded.

Habitat: Open savannah, where it is partial to thorn trees.

Habits: Diurnal. Primarily arboreal. Sleeps in a tree hollow at night, or in a concealed place. Breeding males nod their heads when displaying.

Diet: Invertebrates, including grasshoppers, beetles, and, especially, ants and termites.

Common and regularly seen in Kruger, this unmistakable lizard has the ability to change in appearance depending on its circumstances. During display, the male's head becomes bright blue, but is dull and camouflaged when under threat. Southern Tree Agamas venture onto the ground to find food, but immediately run back to a tree when alarmed. If threatened, they will either bite or open their mouths, showing a startling orange mouth lining. These defence mechanisms are particularly important as, unlike some other lizards, agamas are unable to shed their tails (see *page 156*). (see *page 156*)
Birds of prey are their main predators.

Females and immatures are cryptically patterned.

☐ Rainbow Skink *Trachylepis margaritifera*

Size: TL 18–24 cm

Key identification features: Slender, long-limbed skink. Colour varies depending on age and gender. Young have three prominent pale (yellow or orange) dorsal stripes on dark body, and an electric blue tail. Adult females usually retain this pattern, but stripes may become indistinct. Adult males lose the striped patterning and the dark coppery back becomes stippled with creamy flecks. Older males develop a creamy throat and copper-orange tail.

Habitat: Rocky outcrops in savannah.

Habits: Diurnal. Mature males are highly territorial.

Diet: Insects and other invertebrates.

This beautiful little lizard is abundant in suitable habitat throughout Kruger. Each dominant adult male establishes a territory, which it defends against other adult males. They will tolerate the presence of young males, but when these become sexually mature they are aggressively seen off. Females will lay up to 10 eggs, which hatch after about 60 days.

Despite this species' name, only females and juveniles are brightly coloured.

☐ Striped Skink *Trachylepis striata*

Size: TL 18–22 cm

Key identification features: Similar shape to Rainbow Skink but lacks brightly coloured tail. Mostly dark brown with a pale stripe (variably diffuse or prominent) running down either side of the spine from the ridge of the eye to the tail, where they merge. Underside pale. Lobed ear openings are characteristic and often visible.

Habitat: Varied habitats but partial to trees, human dwellings and rocky outcrops.

Habits: Diurnal.

Diet: Small insects and other invertebrates.

SCRAMBLED EGGS
Most of southern Africa's 23 species of *Trachylepis* skink bear live young; only a minority lay eggs.

This small lizard, which is common in Kruger, can be told from other skinks by the two pale stripes that run down its back. They can often be seen basking in the sun in the early mornings in an exposed position, such as on top of a rock or log. When searching for food they move slowly through leaf-litter or over tree stumps. Females give birth to up to nine young during the wet season.

Look for Striped Skinks at hides, picnic areas and in Kruger's camps.

☐ **Variable Skink** *Trachylepis varia*

Size: TL 12–16 cm

Key identification features: Medium-sized, slender skink with rounded snout. Coloration is variable, ranging from black to olive and brownish, but consistently has two pale stripes along each side.

Habitat: Varied, prefers rocks and tree bases in rock-strewn savannah.

Habits: Diurnal. Darts out from under leaves and rocks to catch prey.

Diet: Insects, spiders and occasionally other lizards.

The Variable Skink is a small lizard with two white stripes along its sides. It is common in Kruger, and likes to bask in the sun in a prominent position on a rock or tree trunk in the early morning, but quickly scuttles to cover when disturbed. Females give birth to up to five young in the wet season from November to March.

LIZARD LIFE

Lizards are cold-blooded and so need to regulate their body temperature. To warm up they will bask, lying perpendicular to the sun with their rib cage expanded to maximise the surface area exposed to the sunlight. To cool off, they will either retreat into the shade, open their mouth to increase evaporative cooling, or take refuge in a cool sand burrow. Lizards have a specialized nasal chamber (called the Jacobson's organ) that is highly sensitive to particular odours. When you see a lizard fluttering its throat, it is essentially 'tasting the air' by increasing the air-flow over this organ to detect potential prey or danger.

TAKE MY TAIL!

Many species of skink and gecko can shed part of their tail when they are captured. The detached tail continues to wriggle, distracting the predator, thus giving the lizard a chance to flee. If the tail has not been consumed by the predator, the lizard may return and eat it itself, thereby retaining some of its own resources. Over a period of weeks the lizard can regenerate its tail, although the new tail may be slimmer and a different colour to the rest of the body.

Common Tropical House Gecko *Hemidactylus mabouia*
(Moreau's Tropical House Gecko)

Size: TL 12–16 cm

Key identification features: Medium-sized gecko with long, pointed snout, large eyes and vertical pupils. Greyish back has dark cross-band markings, belly is paler.

Habitat: Woodland, hiding in crevices under the loose bark of trees during the day. Also seen regularly in buildings in rest camps.

Habits: Nocturnal. Gives a *"tic-tic-tic"* vocalization, often repeated 7–8 times.

Diet: Crickets, moths, beetles, cockroaches, spiders and scorpions.

One of 13 species of gecko in Kruger, this small lizard is abundant and found in most rest camps, where it has a habit of hunting near lights that attract its insect prey. It is extremely territorial, and dominant males will fight vigorously with any interlopers, arching their back, opening their mouth and even biting. If attacked by predators they are able to detach their tail (see *opposite*). Two eggs are laid in dark crevices.

GECKO FUN FACTS
Southern Africa has a diverse gecko fauna, with over 111 species recorded and several others yet to be formally described. Geckos have large eyes but are unable to move their eyelids, and so cannot blink: to clean their eyes they lick them with their tongue. Most geckos have pads on the soles of their feet that are made up of minute hairs which adhere strongly to microscopic irregularities on seemingly smooth surfaces. This enables them to exploit habitats unavailable to other lizards. Geckos are also the only lizards with vocal chords, making grunting and clicking sounds at night to advertise their presence. Geckos shed their skin as they mature and when they do so, they eat it – with nothing going to waste!

☐ Common Giant Plated Lizard *Matobosaurus validus*

Size: TL 40–60 cm

Key identification features: Large, flattened lizard with blunt snout, chunky legs and stubby toes, like a mini bull-necked monitor (*pages 146–147*). Body mostly dark brown with dense olive mottling. Throat is whitish. Breeding male's head becomes tinged pinkish.

Habitat: Rocky outcrops, preferring huge granite boulders in savannah.

Habits: Diurnal and terrestrial. Shy and mostly solitary.

Diet: Invertebrates, small vertebrates including other lizards, and plant matter including flowers and fruits.

Common Giant Plated Lizards have an ingenious defence mechanism: when threatened, they squeeze themselves into a tight rock crevice and inflate their body; in this way they are almost impossible to prise out.

Second only to monitor lizards in terms of size and weight, the Common Giant Plated Lizard is a fairly common species in Kruger in suitable rocky habitat. It differs from Rough-scaled Plated Lizard, which can occur in similar habitat, by its larger size and the lack of keeled scales. The female lays up to five eggs in a rocky crevice, which are then covered with soil. After hatching, the young remain with their parents, forming small family groups. There appears to be some level of parental care and a complex social structure, with individuals being able to recognize other family members.

☐ Rough-scaled Plated Lizard *Broadleysaurus major*

Size: TL 30–40 cm

Key identification features: Stout and flattened like Common Giant Plated Lizard, with chunky legs and stubby toes, but smaller and much yellower with honey-coloured body and limbs mottled with dark brown. Long, yellowish flank stripe down the mid-side. Chin and throat pale yellow.

Juveniles are more boldly patterned than adults.

Habitat: Savannah near rocky outcrops, or places that provide suitable hiding places (*e.g.* termitaria or cavities between tree roots).

Habits: Diurnal and terrestrial. Shy and solitary, seldom in groups.

Diet: Fruits, insects, millipedes, reptiles.

This medium-sized lizard is common in the southern half of Kruger, but rare farther north. Its smaller size and the presence of keeled scales differentiates it from the Common Giant Plated Lizard. Although Rough-scaled Plated Lizards favour rocky crevices or termite mounds, they sometimes dig their own burrows in open savannah. They will also dig actively into soft ground when searching for food. Courtship and breeding occur in late winter (July–August), the female laying up to six eggs in a crack in a rock or log; the eggs hatch around 75 days later. When attacked by predators these lizards are able to shed their tail (see *page 156*).

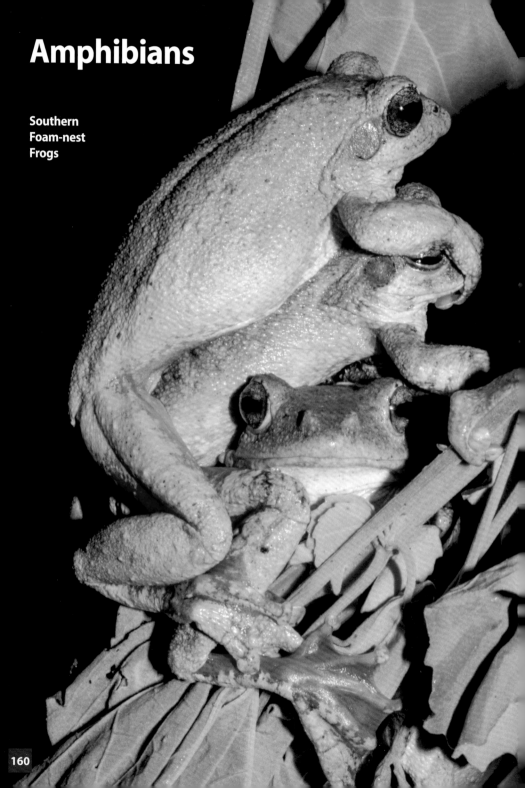

Amphibians

**Southern
Foam-nest
Frogs**

This section covers eight of around 35 amphibian species recorded in Kruger. Your best chance of finding a frog is in the safety of a fenced rest camp after dark, particularly after heavy rain during the wet season (November–March). Never be tempted to explore water bodies of any sort in Kruger, as there are likely to be dangerous animals such as crocodiles and Hippos about.

AMAZING METAMORPHOSIS

In most frog species, eggs are laid in the water, and when tadpoles hatch they are entirely aquatic. They have gills and a tail like a fish, and mostly eat vegetable matter using a small, enclosed mouth. When environmental conditions are suitable, the metamorphosis process will begin. Lungs, legs and jaws grow, while the mouth, gills, spiral gut and tail are re-absorbed. When complete, an aquatic herbivore has transformed into a terrestrial predator. It is one of the most amazing transitions in the animal world!

AESTIVATION

To survive the dry season in Kruger most frogs enter a state of dormancy, known as aestivation, lowering their metabolic rate to retain water and conserve energy. They do this having first sealed themselves in a cavity underground or in a tree, sometimes in a cocoon. Once the rains arrive in October–November, at the beginning of the wet season, the animals become active again.

African Bullfrog

161

■ African Bullfrog *Pyxicephalus edulis*
(Edible Bullfrog)

Size: TL 90–120 mm (♂ smaller than ♀)

Key identification features: Large, plump, green to brown frog with short legs and yellow throat (male) or white throat (female). Upper surface is covered in rough, whitish, glandular ridges or spots. It has three tooth-like projections on the lower jaw.

Habitat: Flooded grassland and rain-filled pools in the wet season.

Habits: Lives in a burrow when active. Spends up to 10 months of the year dormant (aestivating) underground (see *page 161*). Gives a dog-like, yapping call "*waap, waap...*".

Diet: Invertebrates and small vertebrates, including frogs and birds.

This huge frog is uncommon in Kruger, and only seen when breeding is stimulated by heavy rains filling shallow seasonal pans during the wet season. It could be confused with the much rarer **Giant Bullfrog** *Pyxicephalus adspersus* (not illustrated), but is separated by a usually conspicuous white spot on the depressed external ear (tympanum). If conditions are unfavourable and food in short supply, juvenile African Bullfrogs can turn cannibalistic. Bullfrogs most often fall prey to monitor lizards.

BULLFROG REMEDIES
The reason the African Bullfrog was given the scientific name *edulis*, is that it is considered by some people to be edible. They are also often used by local people in traditional medicine.

◼ Southern Foam-nest Frog *Chiromantis xerampelina*
(Grey Foam-nest Treefrog)

Size: TL ♂ 50–75 mm, ♀ 60–90 mm
Key identification features: Fingers on front feet in opposing pairs, enabling the adhesive toepads to grip. Warty skin brownish to grey but may turn almost white in daylight to reduce light absorption. The pupils are horizontal.
Habitat: Trees and structures (including man-made) overhanging savannah pans.
Habits: Primarily nocturnal, calls are made by male only. Secretes a waterproof cocoon and aestivates inderground during the dry season (see *page 161*)
Diet: Insects and other invertebrates.

The Southern Foam-nest Frog is easily identified by unique sucker-like lobes on its toes and fingers. It is common, but most often seen during the wet season. At the first rains these medium-sized frogs emerge from dry-season resting chambers and produce remarkable 'out-of-water' foam-nests, located on overhanging branches. The female creates the foam by rubbing her hind legs together, turning a liquid secreted from her cloaca (urogenital opening) into a froth. Into this foam she lays up to 1,000 eggs, which are fertilized by males (sometimes up to 12) which gather to join in the orgy. The outer foam hardens, preventing desiccation and protecting the developing tadpoles from predation. About five days after hatching the tadpoles wriggle through the foam and drop into the water below. This frog has various adaptations that enable it to tolerate high temperatures and minimize water loss during the dry season. For example, it can secrete water droplets through the skin to cool down (similar to human sweating), and conserves water by producing semi-solid waste instead of urine.

Look for the distinctive foam nests overhanging temporary pools in the wet season.

■ Banded Rubber Frog *Phrynomantis bifasciatus*

Size: TL 50–65 mm

Key identification features: Shiny black frog with two prominent red-orange stripes along back, and red spots on legs and flanks; grey with white spots below.

Habitat: Savannah pans and adjacent hollows in logs or cover.

Habits: Nocturnal. Walks rather than jumps. Gives a high-pitched, bird-like "*prrrrr*" trill at night.

Diet: Mainly eats ants, impervious to the formic acid that deters other predators. Also eats termites and other invertebrates.

The unmistakable Banded Rubber Frog is the only boldly marked red-and-black frog in the region. It is fairly common and widespread in Kruger and most often seen during the wet season. Breeding occurs in temporary pools, and males may gather in large groups and call in chorus after rain. The frog's skin is smooth and dry and feels like rubber when handled, hence its name.

APOSEMATISM

Some animals advertise to potential predators that they taste awful, are poisonous, and are best avoided. The term for this is aposematism (or 'warning signal', derived from the Greek words *apo* = away + *sema* = sign). The Banded Rubber Frog's striking coloration is a strong warning to predators that it exudes a particularly potent toxin from its glandular skin; rashes, respiratory difficulties and nausea have all resulted from ingestion and absorption of this toxin. To deter predators, a threatened frog will also arch-up, making itself appear larger. However, neither of these measures seems to deter some birds (such as Hamerkop *Scopus umbretta*) from eating it with impunity.

☐ Snoring Puddle Frog *Phrynobatrachus natalensis*
(Natal Dwarf Puddle Frog)

Size: TL 25–30 mm

Key identification features: Squat with a pointed snout; brownish, mottled. Similar to **Dwarf Puddle Frog** *Phrynobatrachus mababiensis* (not illustrated), with which it is easily confused as both species are fairly common in Kruger, but larger, with strongly webbed toes (webbing absent in Dwarf Puddle Frog).

Habitat: Herbaceous vegetation along rivers and in marshes, pans and flooded grassland.

Habits: Both diurnal and nocturnal. Aggressive territorial encounters between males are commonplace. Call is a nasal snoring, not buzzing and clicking like Dwarf Puddle Frog. Aestivates underground in the dry season (see *page 161*).

Diet: Invertebrates, including insects, earthworms and snails; also other frogs.

The Snoring Puddle Frog is fairly common and widespread in Kruger, most often seen during the wet season. It is often confused with the **Dwarf Puddle Frog** (see *Key identification features*). The coloration is variable across Africa, and there is a strong possibility that the Snoring Puddle Frog is, in fact, more than one species that are so similar in appearance that they cannot be told apart without resorting to DNA analysis (these are known as 'cryptic species'). However, within Kruger, the colour variation is more likely related to camouflage. It breeds in temporary pools after rain and is preyed upon by snakes, other reptiles and birds.

☐ Bubbling Kassina *Kassina senegalensis*
(Senegal Land Frog)

Size: TL 33–49 mm

Key identification features: Flattish frog with raised eye-sockets and large, brownish eyes with a vertically slit 'cats-eye' pupil. Tips of toes and fingers are expanded into small disks. Coloration is variable, but most individuals in Kruger are olive, with a bold brown stripe down the spine, blotches on the body, flanks and legs, and dark face patch.

Habitat: Temporary and permanent pools in savannah and grassland.

Habits: Males call from concealed positions near the water's edge. Prefers to walk and run, rather than hop. The call is a popping "*quoip*".

Diet: Invertebrates, including insects and spiders.

Most often seen during the wet season, this small- to medium-sized frog is fairly common and widespread in Kruger. The rarer **Red-legged Kassina** *Kassina maculata* is superficially similar but is spotted rather than striped on the back and has red suffusion on the groin and armpits. The coloration of both species is variable – either as a camouflage-related adaptation or possibly because, as with the Snoring Puddle Frog (*page 165*) more than one 'cryptic species' is involved. Males gather together after rain and a 'bubbling' chorus ripples across the night; one of Africa's characteristic sounds. The eggs are laid underwater, adhered to vegetation. The tadpoles are distinctively marked with red or golden markings, and have high tail fins. This frog often falls prey to snakes.

☐ Plain Grass Frog *Ptychadena anchietae*
(Anchieta's Ridged Frog)

Size: TL ♂ 40–50 mm, ♀ 62 mm

Key identification features: Wide head, pointed snout, long legs. Fingers lack webbing, but toes well-webbed. Horizontal pupil. Distinctive ridges (six or more) on the upperside. Back pinkish-red; legs olive-brown. Pale triangle covers the upper snout. Similar species in Kruger include **Broad-banded Grass Frog** *P. mossambica* and **Sharp-nosed Grass Frog** *P. oxyrhynchus* (neither illustrated). The three are separated by comparing the relative distance between the openings of their nostrils with the distance from the end of the snout to the nostrils:

Plain Grass Frog: same
Broad-banded Grass Frog: greater
Sharp-nosed Grass Frog: less.

Habitat: Open country in woodland, grassland and forest, near, but often not in, permanent water.

Habits: Nocturnal. Agile jumper. Highly vocal during the wet season. The call is a high-pitched trill.

Diet: Invertebrates, including insects like grasshoppers and beetles.

This medium-sized frog is fairly common and widespread in Kruger, and most often seen during the wet season. Although the Plain Grass Frog is the commonest grass frog in Kruger, there are two other similar species – and making a certain identification is difficult unless close views are obtained (see *Key identification features*). Mating takes place on vegetation just above the water surface, and as the eggs emerge the male uses his back legs to funnel his sperm onto them, improving the chances of fertilization.

■ Bushveld Rain Frog *Breviceps adspersus*
(Common Rain Frog)

Size: TL ♂ 30–47 mm, ♀ 40–60 mm

Key identification features: Globular, short-legged, brownish-green, pug-faced frog. The only rain frog (*Breviceps*) in most of Kruger; cannot jump, and has stumpy legs on which it walks awkwardly. Facial features look shrunken, with a small 'unhappy' mouth and beady eyes.

Habitat: Woodland with damp, sandy soils.

Habits: Entirely terrestrial; cannot swim. In the dry winter months, burrows 20 cm under the surface, where it aestivates (see *page 161*), sometimes communally. After rain, males emerge and call near their burrow, defending their territory; they are largely solitary. Mostly nocturnal, but will call during the day if it is wet and dark enough; the call is a short whistle.

Diet: Mostly termites (including winged alates), ants and other invertebrates.

This pudgy frog is fairly common and widespread in Kruger, and most often seen during the wet season. The similar **Mozambique Rain Frog** *B. mossambicus* is found only on the park's western border, where it is very rare. Using an adhesive secretion, male Bushveld Rain Frogs attach themselves to the larger females during nest construction, fertilizing her eggs as they are deposited in a chamber she has dug 30 cm below the soil surface. In an amazing adaptation to a terrestrial lifestyle, the tadpole stage is bypassed, with the eggs of this species hatching into froglets. If threatened, Bushveld Rain Frogs inflate their body and produce a noxious milky secretion as an anti-predatory mechanism. Despite this, they still regularly fall prey to birds and mammals.

Painted Reed Frog *Hyperolius marmoratus*
(Marbled Reed Frog)

Most often seen during the wet season, this small frog is fairly common and widespread in Kruger. Despite being extremely variable in coloration, it is easily recognized, as all the other species of reed frogs in Kruger are green. Males call from waterside vegetation such as reeds and sedges, and individuals will return to the same site each evening. They are good jumpers, and expose red skin on their thighs when they leap, which acts to startle predators; nevertheless, they are still taken by birds, snakes, young crocodiles, terrapins and other frogs.

Size: TL 25–35 mm

Key identification features: Colour pattern is highly variable, but in Kruger the race *taeniatus* tends to be a spectacular black, yellow (occasionally red) and white striped frog. The side of the snout is curved.

Habitat: Temporary and permanent ponds in savannah.

Habits: Breeds from October to February, but calls at any time. Ascends vegetation during the day, using well-developed toe-pads, but returns to the pond at night to call; the male's call is a loud, short whistle. Aestivates during the dry season (see *page 161*) under logs or stones, or amongst dense vegetation.

Diet: Invertebrates, including insects.

The Painted Reed Frog is highly variable in colour and pattern

Further reading

This book focuses on the mammals, reptiles and amphibians you are most likely to see during a visit to Kruger National Park. However, if you find something that you cannot identify, do not despair: there are separate, comprehensive, books that cover all the species in each of these groups found in the region. A selection of the best is listed below, together with other suggestions for further reading to enhance your visit.

Mammals

Stuarts' Field Guide to Mammals of Southern Africa (2015) by C. and M. Stuart. Struik.

The Safari Companion: A Guide to Watching African Mammals (2000) by R. D. Estes. Chelsea Green.

Beat About the Bush: Mammals and Birds (2013) by T. Carnaby. Jacana Media.

Reptiles and amphibians

A Guide to the Reptiles of Southern Africa (2007) by G. Alexander and J. Marais. Struik.

A Complete Guide to the Frogs of Southern Africa (2009) by L. du Preez and V. Carruthers. Struik.

General

Birds of Kruger National Park (2016) by K. Barnes and K. Behrens. Princeton **WILD**Guides

Kruger National Park: Questions and Answers (2014) by P. F. Fourie, updated by C. van der Linde. Struik.

Online resources

The following websites are also worth reviewing before, and if possible, during your visit:

www.latestsightings.com
Fabulous community of shared information regarding real-time sightings of what is being seen in Kruger National Park, and where; with up-to-the-minute accuracy.

www.sanparks.org
South African National Parks website and booking portal. Invaluable information relating to the park, and also the way to book your own stay.

www.krugerpark.co.za
Your one-stop shop for information on private and self-drive safaris, with extensive updates and facts regarding the park.

https://www.facebook.com/groups/krugerparkearth/
The largest and most active Facebook community, sharing photos, information and stories about Kruger National Park.

South African National Parks (SANParks) main regulations

When visiting any of the South African National Parks (SANParks) it is important to keep in mind that for both your safety, and that of the plants and animals, that the following main regulations must be adhered to at all times. The transgression of any of these rules is considered a serious offence and may result in a fine or prosecution.

1. **IDENTIFICATION** All visitors must ensure that acceptable means of identification (*e.g.* passport, national identity document, or drivers license) are taken along when visiting national parks.

2. **STAY IN YOUR VEHICLE** Within national parks there is a possible threat from dangerous animals, and visitors may only alight from vehicles in designated areas. No part of your body may protrude from the vehicle, and doors should always remain closed.

3. **SPEED LIMIT** Always observe the speed limits applicable.

4. **ALCOHOL** The consumption of alcohol in public areas is prohibited. Day visitors are not permitted to enter national parks with any alcohol.

5. **DRIVE SAFELY** General rules of the road apply. Driving or operating any vehicle without a driver's license, under the influence of alcohol, in a reckless or negligent manner, or in a deliberate disregard for the safety of a person, animal or property is prohibited.

6. **GATE TIMES** Gate times must be strictly adhered to; after hours driving is prohibited.

7. **OVERNIGHT VISITORS** Guests are only permitted to stay at recognized overnight facilities and must report to the relevant reception before occupying accommodation or camping.

8. **AGE RESTRICTIONS** For safety reasons some national parks' activities have age restrictions.

9. **DEPARTURE TIMES** All accommodation and camping sites can be occupied from 14h00 on arrival day and must be vacated by 10h00 on departure day.

10. **DRIVING AREAS** Vehicles must remain on designated roads at all times; off-road driving or driving on closed or no-entry roads is prohibited. Please take careful note of vehicle restrictions (including suitability of caravans/trailers, and/or vehicles exceeding a certain mass, type or size) applicable to the different roads and areas of the national parks.

11. **FEEDING OF WILDLIFE** The feeding or intentional disturbance of wildlife is prohibited. Wildlife that becomes dependent upon human handouts can turn aggressive and often has to be eliminated.

12. **FLORA & FAUNA** No natural (*e.g.* plant or animal) or cultural items may be removed from the park without an official permit. Poaching, killing or injuring of animals, or cutting, damaging or being in possession of any natural item is prohibited. Importing of any invasive species into national parks is also prohibited.

13. **PETS** No pets may be brought into national parks. Guide dogs for visually impaired visitors are an exception, but only following consultation with park management in advance.

14. **LITTER-FREE ZONE** All littering is prohibited.

15. **DECLARE DANGEROUS ITEMS** All firearms/weapons, traps or poison must be declared upon entry into a national park.

16. **FIRE HAZARD** Causing fire, whether intentionally or unintentionally, other than in a rest camp fireplace, is strictly prohibited.

17. **SMOKING** Please obey the smoking regulations applicable.

18. **BEHAVIOUR** Behaving in an offensive, improper, indecent or disorderly manner, including making excessive noise, is strictly prohibited. The obstructing of an authorized official in the execution of his/her duties will not be tolerated.

19. **BEWARE MALARIA** Kruger National Park falls within a malaria zone. A 24-hour malaria hotline is available on +27 (0)82-234-1800.

Rhinos on the edge

About 30% of the world's White and Black Rhinoceroses are found in Kruger National Park. Despite being strictly protected, poaching continues to be a major scourge and these magnificent animals are rapidly disappearing (see *page 85*). If you have just had an unforgettable encounter with a rhino and would like to help ensure that our children and grandchildren have a chance to see these remarkable animals free and in the wild, please consider making a donation to one of the charities listed below:

Breaking the Brand (breakingthebrand. org) attempts to raise awareness of the impacts of wildlife product purchases in user markets. Advertising campaigns have been launched in Vietnam and China aimed at reducing the demand for rhino horn; this approach has been successful in virtually eliminating the use of rhino horn in other Asian countries, such as Japan (1970s), South Korea (1980s) and Taiwan (1990s).

The Endangered Wildlife Trust (EWT) (ewt. org.za) and **WWF South Africa** (wwf.org.za) are South African-based charities that tackle the rhino poaching issue by assisting anti-poaching patrols, translocating rhinos to safer sanctuaries, working with communities on the margins of rhino conservation areas, assisting in the creation of new protected areas, and investigating demand reduction.

The volunteer **SANParks Honorary Rangers** (sanparksvolunteers.org) assist with anti-poaching patrols.

The **International Rhino Foundation** (IRF) (rhinos.org) and **Save the Rhino International** (savetherhino.org) are international organizations working to ensure the survival of the world's rhinos through conservation, research and advocacy.

Kruger National Park supports more **White Rhinos** than any other national park.

Acknowledgements and photo credits

Jen Brumfield prepared all the spoor illustrations for this book. Mark Lorenz and Karen Birkenbach commented on the entire manuscript. Marius Burger was a mountain, both reading the reptile and amphibian texts, and donating a huge number of photos for use in exchange for a Rocky Horror Picture Show ticket. Johan Marais and James Harvey commented on reptile and frog accounts. Iain Campbell and Richard Barnes each joined me in the field for a week, and also contributed their images. My parents, wife and son all had their holidays turned into photo opportunities for the book. Thanks so much for being understanding. To the many photographers whose photos appear on these pages I am indebted, and to the Tropical Birding clients that I have had the privilege of sharing the magnificence of Kruger with, thanks for the good times. The team at **WILD***Guides* – Rob and Rachel Still, Andy and Gill Swash, and Brian Clews – thanks so much for helping make sure the content was there, the details accurate and for designing a beautiful little book. Robert Kirk at Princeton, thanks for believing in this project.

All the images included in this book were taken by the author, apart from the following:

Ken Behrens: Common Slender Mongoose (inset, *p. 66*), African Elephant (*p. 78*). **Marius Burger:** Common Rough-scaled Lizard (*p. 140*), Serrated Hinged Terrapin (*p. 145*), Rock Monitor (*p. 147*), Water Monitor juvenile (*p. 147*), Puff Adder (*p.148*), Mozambique Spitting Cobra (*p. 149*), Black Mamba (*p. 150*), Southern African Python (*p. 151*), Common Flap-necked Chameleon (*p. 152*), Rainbow Skink (both, *p. 154*), Striped Skink (main image, *p. 155*), Variable Skink (*p. 156*), Common Tropical House Gecko (*p. 157*), Common Giant Plated Lizard (main image, *p. 158*), Rough-scaled Plated Lizard (both, *p. 159*), Southern Foam-nest Frog (*pp. 160 & 163*), African Bullfrog (*pp. 161, 162*), Banded Rubber Frog (*p. 164*), Snoring Puddle Frog (*p. 165*), Bubbling Kassina (*p. 166*), Plain Grass Frog (*p. 167*), Bushveld Rain Frog (*p. 168*), Painted Reed Frog (both, *p. 169*). **Iain Campbell:** Hippopotamus (*p. 27*), Leopard (*p. 28*), Cheetah (*p. 48*), Spotted Hyena (bottom, *p. 61*), Black-backed Jackal (*p. 70*), Hippopotamus (inset, *p. 89*). **Luis Casiano / Biosphoto / FLPA:** Spotted-necked Otter (*p. 76*). **Greg and Yvonne Dean**/worldwildlifeimages.com: Aardvark (*p. 75*), Springhare (*p. 129*). **Pat De La Harpe**/naturepl. com: African Clawless Otter (*p. 77*). **Angus Hart**/flickr.com/photos/angushart: Temminck's Ground Pangolin (*p. 74*). **Leon Marais:** Leopard (*p. 44*), Serval (*p. 52*), Side-striped Jackal (*p. 71*). **W.T. Miller / FLPA:** Zorilla (*p. 68*). **Anup Shah**/naturepl.com: Aardwolf (*p. 63*). **Derek Solomon:** Southern Tree Agama (female, *p. 153*). **Andy and Gill Swash**/worldwildlifeimages.com: Common Genet (*p. 56*). **Warwick Tarboton**/warwicktarboton.co.za: African Civet (*p. 55*), Large Spotted Genet (*p. 57*), White-tailed Mongoose (*p. 67*), Thick-tailed Greater Galago (*p. 137*). **S Watson:** Water Monitor (head, *p. 147*).

In addition, the following images are licensed under a Creative Commons Attribution-ShareAlike 2.0 UK: England & Wales License:

Nebit Dilman: Fever Tree (*p. 19*). **Bernard Dupont:** Red Grass (*p. 18*); figs on Sycamore, Sausage Tree, Sausage Tree fruits, Wild Date Palm, Wild Date Palm fruit, riverine forest (all, *p. 19*); broadleaved woodland (*pp. 20–21*); Large-fruited Bushwillow, Large-fruited Bushwillow fruit, Silver Cluster-leaf, Silver Cluster-leaf fruit, Russet Bushwillow, Russet Bushwillow fruit (all, *p. 20*); Mopane, Mopane leaves, Baobab, Sickle Bush, Sickle Bush flower, Marula, Marula fruits (all *p. 21*). **Richard Gill:** Sycamore Fig (*p. 19*). **Steve Jurvetson:** King Cheetah (*p. 51*). **JMK:** Digit Grass, Knobthorn, Knobthorn flower (all, *p. 18*); Red Bushwillow, Red Bushwillow fruit (both, *p. 19*). **Derek Keats:** Grassland plains (*p. 18*). **Kip Lee:** Baobab flower (*p. 21*). **Vaughan Lieberum:** Common Wildebeest (inset, *p. 127*). **Forest and Kim Starr:** Buffalo Grass (*p. 18*). **Tatters:** Weeping Boer-bean; Weeping Boer-bean seeds and flowers (both, *p. 19*).

Index

This index includes the common English and scientific (*in italics*) names of all the mammals, reptiles and amphibians mentioned mentioned in this book.

Bold text is used to highlight the main species accounts.

Italicized numbers indicate other page(s) on which a photograph appears.

Blue figures relate to the mammal track (spoor) illustrations.

Regular text is used for species that are not subject to a full account.

A
Aardvark 33, **75**
Aardwolf 34, **62**
Acanthocercus atricollis **153**
Acinonyx jubatus **48**
Adder, Puff **148**
Aepyceros melampus **122**
Agama, Southern Tree **153**
Anteater, Scaly
    (see Temminck's Ground Pangolin) **74**
Antelope, Roan 39, **116**
—, Sable 39, **118**
Antilocapra americana 94
Aonyx capensis **77**

B
Baboon, Chacma 37, **134**
Badger, Honey 36, **69**
Bitis arietans **148**
Bongo 112
Breviceps adspersus **168**
— *mossambicus* 168
Broadleysaurus major **159**
Buffalo, African 38, **98**
Bullfrog, African (or Edible) *161*, **162**
—, Giant 162
Bushbaby, Greater
    (see Thick-tailed Greater Galago) **137**
—, **Lesser** (see Southern Lesser Galago) ... **136**
Bushbuck 39, **112**

C
Canis adustus **71**
— *mesomelas* **70**
Caracal 35, **53**
Caracal caracal **53**
Cat, Wild 35, **54**
Cavia porcellus 130
Ceratotherium simum **82**
Chamaeleo dilepis **152**

Chameleon, Common Flap-necked **152**
Cheetah 8, 35, **48**
Chiromantis xerampelina **163**
Chlorocebus pygerythrus **132**
Choeropsis liberiensis 89
Civet, African 35, **55**
Civettictis civetta **55**
Cobra, Mozambique Spitting **149**
—, Snouted 149
Connochaetes taurinus **126**
Crocodile, Nile **142**
—, Saltwater 142
Crocodylus niloticus **142**
— *porosus* 142
Crocuta crocuta **58**

D
Damaliscus lunatus **124**
Dassie, Rock (see Rock Hyrax) **130**
Dendroaspis polylepis **150**
Diceros bicornis **84**
Dog, African Wild (or Cape Hunting) 34, **72**
Dugong **130**
Dugong dugon 130
Duiker, Common (or Bush, or Grey) ... 39, **106**

E
Eland, Common 39, **102**
—, Giant 102
Elephant, African *10–11*, 16, *24*, 32, **78**
Epomophorus **139**
— *crypturus* 139
— *wahlbergi* 139
Equus quagga **92**

F
Felis sylvestris **54**
Frog, Anchieta's Ridged (see Plain Grass Frog) ... **167**
—, **Banded Rubber** **164**
—, Broad-banded Grass 167

Frog, Bushveld (or Common) Rain 168
—, Dwarf Puddle 165
—, Marbled Reed (see Painted Reed Frog) 169
—, Mozambique Rain 168
—, Natal Dwarf Puddle
   (see Snoring Puddle Frog) 165
—, Painted Reed 169
—, Plain Grass 167
—, Senegal Land (see Bubbling Kassina) 166
—, Sharp-nosed Grass 167
—, Snoring Puddle 165
—, Southern Foam-nest *160*, 163
Fruit-bat, Epauletted 139
—, Peters's 139
—, Wahlberg's 139

G
Galago moholi 136
Galago, Large-eared Greater
   (see Thick-tailed Greater Galago) 137
—, Mohol (see Southern Lesser Galago) 136
—, South African (see Southern Lesser Galago) .. 136
—, Southern Lesser 37, 136
—, Thick-tailed Greater 37, 137
Gecko, Common (or Moreau's) Tropical House .. 157
Genet, Common 36, 56
—, Large-spotted 36, 57
Genetta genetta 56
— *maculata* 57
Giraffa camelopardalis 94
Giraffe 36, 94
Gnu (see Common Wildebeest) 126
Grysbok, Limpopo (see Sharpe's Grysbok) 107
—, Sharpe's 30, 39, 107

H
Hare, African Savannah 128
—, Scrub 33, 128
—, Spring (see Springhare) 33, 129
Helogale parvula 65
Hemidactylus mabouia 157
Herpestes sanguineus 66
Hippopotamus 27, 32, 86
—, Pygmy 89
Hippopotamus amphibious 86
Hippotragus equinus 116
— *niger* 118
Hydrictis maculicollis 76
Hyena, Spotted 34, 58
Hyperolius marmoratus 169
Hyrax, Rock 33, 130
Hystrix africaeaustralis 131

I
Ichneumia albicauda 67
Ictonyx striatus 68
Imbabala (see Bushbuck) 112
Impala 39, 122

J
Jackal, Black-backed 34, 70
—, Side-striped 34, 71

K
Kassina maculata 166
— *senegalensis* 166
Kassina, Bubbling 166
—, Red-legged 166
Kinixys belliana 144
— *spekii* 144
Klipspringer 38, 109
Kobus ellipsiprymnus 120
Kudu, Greater 39, 104

L
Leopard 28, 31, 35, 44
Leptailurus serval 52
Lepus microtis 128
— *saxatilis* 128
Lion *1*, 25, 35, 40
Lizard, Common Giant Plated 158
—, Common Rough-scaled *141*
—, Rough-scaled Plated 159
Loxodonta africana 78
Lycaon pictus 72

M
Mamba, Black 150
Manatee 130
Matobosaurus validus 158
Meroles squamulosus *141*
Mellivora capensis 69
Mongoose, Banded 37, 64
—, Common Dwarf 37, 65
—, Common Slender 37, 66
—, White-tailed 36, 67
Monitor, Rock 146
—, Water 146
Monkey, Vervet 37, 132
Mungos mungo 64

N
Naja annulifera 149
— *mossambica* 149
Nyala 39, 114

O

Okapi 94
Okapia johnstoni 94
Oreotragus oreotragus **109**
Orycteropus afer 75
Otolemur crassicaudatus **137**
Otter, African (or Cape) Clawless 33, **77**
—, **Spotted-necked** 33, **76**

P

Pangolin, Temminck's Ground 33, **74**
Panthera leo **40**
— *pardus* **44**
Papio ursinus **134**
Paraxerus cepapi **138**
Pedetes capensis **129**
Pelomedusa subrufa 145
Pelusios sinuatus 145
Phacochoerus africanus **90**
Phrynobatrachus mababiensis 165
— *natalensis* 165
Phrynomantis bifasciatus **164**
Pig, Guinea 130
Poecilogale albinucha 68
Polecat, Striped (see Zorilla) 36, **68**
Porcupine, Cape 33, **131**
Procavia capensis **130**
Pronghorn 94
Proteles cristata **62**
Ptychadena anchietae **167**
— *mossambica* 167
— *oxyrhynchus* 167
Python natalensis **151**
Python, Southern African **151**
Pyxicephalus adspersus 162
— *edulis* **162**

R

Raphicerus campestris **108**
— *colonicus* 107
— *sharpei* 107
Ratel (see Honey Badger) **69**
Redunca arundinum **110**
— *fulvorufula* 110
Reedbuck, Common (see Southern Reedbuck) 110
—, **Mountain** 110
—, **Southern** 39, **110**
Rhinoceros, Black 32, **84**
—, **Hooked-lipped** (see Black Rhinoceros) 84
—, **Square-lipped** (see White Rhinoceros) 82
—, **White** 29, 32, **82**, *172*

S

Serval 33, **52**
Sitatunga 106
Skink, Rainbow **154**
—, **Striped** **155**
—, **Variable** **156**
Smutsia temminckii **74**
Springhare 33, **129**
Squirrel, Smith's Bush 33, **138**
—, **Tree** (see Smith's Bush Squirrel) 138
Steenbok 39, **108**
Stigmochelys pardalis **144**
Sylvicapra grimmia 106
Syncerus caffer **98**

T

Terrapin, Central Marsh 145
—, **Serrated Hinged** 145
Topi (see Tsessebe) **124**
Tortoise, Bell's Hinged 144
—, **Leopard** **144**
—, Speke's Hinged 144
Trachylepis margaritifer **154**
— *striata* 155
— *varia* 156
Tragelaphus angasii **114**
— *derbianus* 102
— *eurycerus* 112
— *oryx* **102**
— *scriptus* 112
— *spekii* 112
— *strepsiceros* **104**
— *sylvaticus* 112
Treefrog, Grey Foam-nest
    (see Southern Foam-nest Frog) **163**
Trichechus 130
Tsessebe *30, 38,* **124**

V

Varanus albigularis **146**
— *niloticus* **146**
Vervet 37, **132**

W

Warthog, Common 38, **90**
Waterbuck 39, **120**
Weasel, African 68
Wildebeest, Common
    (or Blue or White-bearded) 39, **126**
Wolf, Painted (see African Wild Dog) **72**

Z

Zebra, Plains 38, **92**
Zorilla 36, **68**